Columbanus

Poet, Preacher, Statesman, Saint

Carol Richards

imprint-academic.com

Published in the UK by
Imprint Academic, PO Box 200, Exeter EX5 5YX, UK

Published in the USA by
Imprint Academic, Philosophy Documentation Center
PO Box 7147, Charlottesville, VA 22906-7147, USA

ISBN-13: 978184540 190 0

A CIP catalogue record for this book is available from the
British Library and US Library of Congress

Passages from Cardinal Tómas O'Fiaich, *Columbanus in his Own
Words*, Veritas Publications, Dublin, 1974/1990; used with permission.

Copyright material from *The History of the Franks* by Gregory of
Tours, translated with and Introduction by Lewis Thorpe,
Penguin Classics, 1974; used with permission.

Quotations from *Ecclesiastical History of the English People*, edited
by Judith McClure & Roger Collins, OUP, 1999; by permission of
Oxford University Press.

Quotations from *Lost Scriptures*, by Bart D. Ehrman, OUP, 2003;
by permission of Oxford University Press, Inc.

Contents

	A Prayer from St Columbanus	iv
1	Columbanus: Father of the European Union	1
2	Early Life	4
3	The Egyptian Influence	19
4	Christian Druidism	40
5	Why did Columbanus leave Ireland?	54
6	When did Columbanus leave Ireland?	63
7	The Sons of Lothar	83
8	The Nero and Herod of Our Times	91
9	Who Murdered King Chilperic?	102
10	Backwoodsmen	113
11	Rule and Penitential	129
12	The Perfect Diplomat	139
13	Shipwreck	156
14	The Constant Sea	172
15	A New Start	186
16	The Road to Rome	193
17	The Fame of Mortal Life	205
	References	213
	Index	215

A Prayer from St Columbanus

Grant, O Lord, that the light of your love
may never be dimmed within us.
Let it shine forth from our warmed hearts to comfort others
in times of peace and in seasons of adversity
and in bright beams of your goodness and love
may we come at last to the vision of your glory
through Christ our Lord. Amen.

Chapter 1

Columbanus

Father of the European Union

> ... to live without offence, each retaining what he has received and "remaining wherein he has been called".
>
> *Columbanus,*
> *Letter to the newly elected Pope (604 or 607 AD)* [1]

In seeking to explain the concept of modern European unity one of its founding fathers, Monsieur Robert Schuman, described a sixth century wandering Irish monk as "the patron saint of those who seek to construct a united Europe" (Lehane, 2005).

He was speaking of the saint known as Columbanus —although he referred to himself as Columba—which in Latin means "The Dove" —the Latin suffix was added later to distinguish him from his older contemporary Columba of Iona, whom for the sake of convenience we will hereafter refer to by his other name Columcille ("The Dove of the Church").

The addition of the suffix to the name of Columba the Younger as he is also sometimes known indicates that a century after their deaths their lives had already become some-

---

[1]   "This is what the holy fathers, namely Polycarp and Pope Anicetus taught—to live without offence to the faith, nay persevering in perfect charity—each retaining what he has received and 'remaining wherein he has been called'" (O'Fiaich, 1990, p. 77). Cf. St Paul: "Let every man abide in the same calling wherein he was called" (*1 Corinthians* 7.20).

what confused.[2] It is instructive that both men chose the same monastic name because the chances are they left Ireland under very similar circumstances to redeem themselves in missionary activities.

However, what we do know for certain is, that Columcille searched for his redemption in the western isles of Scotland and that significantly he did not go very far from Ireland or exile himself for life. Columbanus, on the other hand, went into permanent exile *in peregrinatione*. In the context of the life of a saint this is usually translated as "on pilgrimage" but *peregrinaggio*[3] – the Italian form of the word – is also translated as "travels and adventures" a description that might be better applied to the story of Columbanus' life, although the spiritual element was never far from the surface, and one which might be of more use to us when examining the motives behind his mission.

His travels and adventures, in the course of a long life, took him from Brittany in the west right up the Rhine valley across the Swiss Alps into Lombardy – what is now northern Italy – finally coming to rest at Bobbio where, after creating his last foundation, he died at the age of seventy, for the time a very old man.

He was therefore the epitome of the "wandering monks" who carried across Europe their brand of Celtic Christianity which, even more interestingly, came back by more or less the same route many centuries later in the form of the Protestant Reformation.

For us, Columbanus holds the secret to the intellectual and spiritual schism that lies at the heart of the Europe M. Schuman[4] was so keen to unite. For many centuries attempts have been made to create a united Europe. Many

---

[2]   To further confuse matters another Columba the Younger was also among the group that accompanied Columbanus.

[3]   Cf the 1557 Venetian book *Peregrinaggio di tre giovani figlivoli del Re di Serendippo* by Christofero Armeno translated as "The Travels and Adventures of Three Princes of Serendip" (Merton & Barber, Princeton, 2004).

[4]   Robert Schuman (1886–1963), a French statesman and a driving force behind the European Coal and Steel Community that developed into the European Union.

times the attempt, however successful for a period, has ultimately failed. Its success or failure, even in the twenty-first century, may equally be laid at the door of this temperamentally volatile itinerant Irishman—typically Irish—a handsome man with a poetic temperament, volcanic temper and a mind rigorous in pursuit of intellectual satisfaction.

Columbanus, as father of the Protestant Reformation, may be said to have destroyed the European unity of the Middle Ages. It's ironic that he is now said to be the inspiration for its unity in its modern form. However, in a sense both claims are perfectly justified as he continues to be revered as a saint by both Protestants and Catholics in roughly equal measures and I will try and unravel this paradox by telling his extraordinary and fascinating story.

Chapter 2

Early Life

Spurn now the sweet deceits of life below
Soft Lust can upright virtue overthrow ...

Columbanus, To Hunaldus [1]

In the first place we should examine what is meant by a saint. Not all saints are martyrs who died for their faith.

A saint in the early days of Christianity was simply someone who belonged to the church—hence the "I believe in the communion of saints" in the Apostles' Creed and the Puritan use of the term to indicate anyone who belonged to their sect.

By the early middle ages the term saint had come to be attached to anyone who had spent a lifetime in the service of Christianity, whether particularly saintly by modern standards or not. In the early lives we find saints indulging in some very unsaintly activities. The extent to which Christianity came to dominate the British Isles is evidenced by the large number of place-names which are dedicated to saints. It became the Land of Saints.

Some of these early saints can with certainty be identified as local pagan deities, spirits of nature, who were translated into Christian saints to legitimise their continued worship, a practice that in itself is consistent with the theology of Christian Druidism,[2] that brand of Christianity peculiar to the British Isles and Northern Europe and quite distinct from Roman Catholicism.

Since there was officially only one western church before the Protestant Reformation, at the outset both versions were

---

[1]   O'Fiaich, 1990, p. 97.
[2]   See Chapter 4.

essentially catholic. In reality, however, there were always two religions — two spiritual tempers — and the schism that took place, although a long time coming was pretty much inevitable.

St Columbanus was among those called a saint because he spent his life dedicated to the pursuit of intellectual excellence in the service of the church, not because he was particularly "saintly" by nature.

Of his early life not much is known. He was born around the year 543 AD somewhere on the Carlow-Wexford border in the south of Ireland (modern Eire).[3]

The society he was born into was based on a rural economy, a world of shepherds, cattle-herders, and, as we know from the tale of the Brown Bull of Cooley, cattle-rustlers.

It was essentially a feudal society ruled by a clutch of petty kings, many probably not much more than provincial chieftains, answerable to an overlord, the Ard Ri — the High King of Ireland — who held his court at Tara.

Below him came a warrior-caste who in turn acted as overlords to their tenants and serfs.

Somewhere in the middle came a professional class of *brehons* who were lawyers and administrators, doctors and most importantly poets.

The poet was not just an entertainer, although he was that too, but also a musician, and music was highly prized in the classical world as a form of higher mathematics. He was also a genealogist — a very important role in a society where everything is based on kinship — and an historian. A poet also had a certain licence to criticise his betters and a notable aspect of his work included the kind of comic verse and satire that later found its apogee in England in Chaucer.

The value placed on the poetic arts may be judged from the fact that poetry was also regarded as a royal, although at

[3]   There is some disagreement regarding his date and place of birth as follows: Lehane, 2005, p. 148, 543AD; Cahill, 1995, p. 188, circa 540AD in Leinster; O'Fiaich, 1990, p. 13, 543 AD on the borders of Carlow and Wexford; Durant, 1950, p. 532, 543 AD in Leinster; *Dictionary of Irish Biography*, ?543 AD; *Oxford Companion to Irish Literature*, ?543 AD born in Leinster; Woods, 2000, "Columban was born about 543 in Leinster somewhere near the Carlow-Wexford border".

that level amateur, art. Both Columbas were accomplished poets as was the King of the Franks. The tradition of the gentleman poet continued well into the seventeenth century but the bards were professionals and, travelling from mead hall to mead hall in search of patronage, they were also an important conduit for communications.

Although as historians we make a clear distinction between the different racial groups of northern Europe and like to treat them as separate entities, this was probably not the case on the ground. The world Columbanus grew up in was very similar to that of the later Anglo-Saxons and Vikings and the neighbouring Franks. So when he went across the Irish Sea and the English Channel to carry his message to the German tribes, the Allemani and the Goths and the Sueves (who are the same people who became Swedes) he would have found himself socially in very familiar territory.

It was not quite the same as say a Victorian Scots missionary heading into Central Africa where he would have encountered a very different type of society from his own.

Nor is it quite accurate to suggest that Ireland, which had not been conquered by the Romans, was entirely free of classical influence.

Although the set-up in Arthur's Britain according to the chronicles we find in Malory was more or less the same as Ireland, the Irish did not have the continuity of settled Roman occupation and administration that we find in Britain and Gaul. Even so, there were strong trading links between the Irish and the British and a constant exchange of personnel and ideas as well as material goods.

In the first half of the fifth century, just before Columbanus was born, both Arthur, the High King of Britain, and the half-British High King of Ireland, Niall of the Nine Hostages as he was known, attempted to follow in the footsteps of Constantine and Maximus and make military expeditions to Rome.[4] In neither case were they successful, the chaos of the Italian peninsula and the onset of plague spreading

---

[4]   Lehane, 2005, p. 37 and Malory, 1996, Bk 5, pp. 128–150

from the Eastern Empire putting an abrupt end to their bids to become Emperor.

Niall, we are told, made it as far as the Alps and was persuaded, probably by a large bribe, by a Roman mission sent to intercept him to return to Ireland. Arthur spent three years in Rome, according to the chronicle, and left prudently just as the plague was reported to be sweeping through Constantinople. Neither of them succeeded in resuscitating the Empire in the West.

However, the fact that they are reported to have made the attempt suggests that the Irish were not as isolated from the rest of Europe as is sometimes claimed. It appears their royal families at least were as much involved in European affairs as everyone else and Niall's half-British ancestry indicates how closely connected the royal families of northern Europe were through intermarriage and kinship ties.

If Columbanus had an aristocratic upbringing and connections with a royal court, it would explain how it is that he exhibits a natural power of command and in his correspondence with popes and kings shows no hint of humility — indeed he might otherwise be regarded as impudent. (He apologises himself for addressing the Pope with "as some call it, my arrogant insolence".)[5]

That it was not regarded so, and that he felt no inclination to seek refuge in deference can probably be explained by the fact that he was of the same social class as his correspondents and so felt no stigma of inferiority when addressing them. He writes to them as equals. Such deference as he manages to summon up is usually tongue-in-cheek. Either he is being humorous or heavily ironic. There's nothing to suggest he meant it.

To such an aristocratic background we could also trace the origin of his formidable diplomatic skills.

---

[5]   Letter to Pope Gregory the Great 600 AD. One must also bear in mind that at this date the Pope was only one of five patriarchs all subject to the jurisdiction of the Eastern Emperor and in no way regarded as infallible or as an absolute monarch; Columbanus, as royalty, may have felt he outranked him.

His habit of command might also be put down to a military training. Unlike monastic foundations in the rest of Britain, where monks were by and large expected to live peacefully, until the ninth century the Irish monks were still required to serve in the military and keep up their martial arts on a daily basis. They were warrior-monks which in the case of both Columbas led to a flashpoint in their careers but must have come in useful when they embarked on missionary activity to essentially warrior-societies.

These wandering monks were battle-hardened men, not wimps. They knew how to take care of themselves.

So from what we know of Columbanus' later career — that he became an Abbot, was a brilliant scholar, an able diplomat and an accomplished poet — we can speculate that he was the younger son of a royal family of Leinster.

The Irish kings, like all the kings of Northern Europe, did not practice primogeniture. A king at the end of his life was expected to divide his estates between his sons and provide for his daughters.

Although on the face of it this appears a fair distribution of their lands and wealth in practice it led to political instability. Either the kingdom became too fragmented to retain economic and military viability and was swallowed up by a stronger neighbour or, more commonly, it led to the sort of murderous family feuds that we will later see erupting among the Frankish kings of mainland Europe.

In Ireland, as elsewhere, this inherent political instability was mitigated slightly by the practice of placing younger sons as novices in the fast growing monasteries paying a substantial "dowry" to ensure that they would one day become Abbot and control the Abbey's considerable estates.[6]

Indeed the practice was partly the cause of their rapid growth. It meant the royal and aristocratic families of the region had a stake in the success of monastic foundations. Brendan Lehane explains,

---

[6] A later Irish saying said a man should have three sons, one to inherit the land, one to go into the church and one to become a poet (i.e. go into one of the professions) which implies dissatisfaction with the way the property had traditionally been divided.

It was not so much simony as a divine right of kingly families. Once under a family's appointment, the abbacy would stay that way, sometimes for as much as five hundred years. From this local patronising there developed a more ambitious empire-building. Monasteries founded, or ostensibly shown to have been founded, by the same man, were grouped in unions of which the most influential abbot became a minor primate (Lehane, 2005, p. 103).

Abbots were powerful landowners, keepers of the important libraries, masters of scholarship and close relatives of kings. They exerted considerable influence and wielded spiritual power quite the equal of that of the temporal and military power of their rulers.

For a young prince it provided a perfect career path, power, status and land which in no way depleted the estates of his family. At the same time it took him out of the line of succession and reduced the danger of sibling rivalry destroying the kingdom. In this way Abbots like the Bishops before them were quite literally princes of the church.

It seems likely that Columbanus was one such little prince.

His *Life* was written (unusually for the time) by a near contemporary, Jonas of Susa, who entered the monastery of Bobbio only three years after Columbanus' death in 615 AD, which makes his account one of the most reliable of early mediaeval hagiographies. Even so, it endows his birth with the usual evidence of divinely ordained predestination customary in the biography of a holy man.

His mother, it is said, dreamed shortly before his birth that the sun rose from her breast and illuminated the whole world with its rays (Jonas, p. 1).

This story, like many a mediaeval biographical detail, is not insignificant "colour" but rather intended to illustrate what makes the individual worthy of note. In Columbanus' case we should focus our attention on his contribution to the enlightenment, not only of the so-called Dark Ages but of all subsequent ages. His mother's prescient image gives us an indication what to look out for.

The year of his birth is worth noting too. Columbanus was born in the same year that the final battle between Arthur and Mordred signalled the end of Romano-Celtic Britain and the beginning of the main Saxon invasion. Britain was changing and the Roman church took full advantage. Along with the Saxons came the papal legate Augustine, also later designated a saint, who appears to have sought to counter the growing influence and strength of the Celtic Church by conspiring with the pagan Saxons.

Augustine is credited with the "conversion" of the English. What did he convert them to? Not Christianity. That had been knocking around the British Isles since the first century AD. The British were already Christian and in large numbers.

At Bangor Iscoed near Wrexham where Augustine was implicated in engineering the massacre of twelve hundred British monks we are told there were two thousand four hundred monks in residence.

Augustine's mission was not to convert the British — nor even the Saxons, since there were more than enough priests in Britain to satisfy their needs — but to curb the influence of Columbanus and the wandering Irish and British monks who were in their turn converting the pagan Germans, Goths and Sueves to their own brand of Christianity, regarded by some members of the Roman church as pernicious and heretical.

To be fair to Pope Gregory, who had sent Augustine to Britain in the first place, after this massacre of Celtic Christians (indignation at which was still being expressed many centuries later, so one can imagine the outrage it must have provoked at the time) he recalled Augustine back to Gaul. Although he was subsequently revered as the Saint of Canterbury, Gregory never allowed him to undertake any missionary work again while he lived. Augustine's companion Laurentius later mentioned Columbanus as an example of uncompromising nonconformity indicating that however much Gregory was annoyed to find Augustine had exceeded the brief he had given him, he was in a manner of speaking acting on orders. The battle lines between Celtic and Roman (and their later manifestations Protestant and Catholic) were already drawn up within the church and the conflict was only just beginning.

The massacre at Bangor Iscoed came towards the end of Columbanus' career so we are jumping ahead here, but it's as well to bear it in mind as we follow the course of his life's journey.

His first studies were at Clun-inis (Cleenish Island) on Lough Erne in Fermanagh. The abbot there was St Sinell, a disciple of Finnian of Clonard, regarded as one of the "Twelve Apostles of Ireland" who taught the other Columba — Columcille.

The influence of Finnian is of great importance not only in relation to the two Columbas but also to the development of the Celtic church throughout the British Isles because he came from St David's and was therefore a Welshman. (Being of Welsh extraction myself, I am bound to point out that Thomas Cahill's title *How the Irish Saved Civilisation* is something of an exaggeration.) In the late fifth and early sixth centuries it was not Ireland but South Wales that was the power-house of Christian scholarship producing a string of great names from Illtud and Cadoc to their pupils Samson of Dol, Paul Aurelian, Gildas and many others who spread their particular version of the gospel throughout most of Britain (apart from the south-east and north of Hadrian's Wall): what is now Wales, Cornwall, Brittany and, following in Patrick's footsteps, Ireland.

Finnian of Clonard was one of this latter generation who had a profound effect on the organisation of the monastic movement in the early sixth century. He had established at Clonard a strict monastic rule derived partly from practices he was accustomed to at St David's. He ate no more than barley bread and water although he allowed himself fish and mead on Sundays as a treat. He never wore anything but a coarse wool habit.

The extent of Finnian's influence, through Sinell, and later Abbot Comgall of Bangor where he went to further his studies, can be judged from Columbanus' own Rule. This work, we are told, shows traces of borrowings "from an

Ireland in the Sixth Century

earlier British or Irish penitential ascribed to Vinnian, possibly a correspondent of Gildas" (Collins, 1999, pp. 240–9).

"Vinnian" is the same as "Finnian". I mentioned he was a Welshman and in Welsh F is pronounced as the English V, except of course there were no Welshman at that date. He was not even necessarily a Celt. South Wales and the area on the other side of the Severn estuary roughly corresponding to modern Somerset and Avon was an area with a strong Roman presence. It was a heady mix of native Celtic, Christian and Classical influences that the "Twelve Apostles" took to Ireland. No one ethnic group can really lay claim to the movement.

Also of interest is the fact that the monastery at Clonard was planned like a hill-fort. When Columbanus set up his first foundation at Annegray the site he chose was that of an abandoned Roman fort. It turned out not to be the best choice in the short-term but the fact that he chose it can probably be traced to the influence of his role-model Finnian of Clonard. All the monasteries seem to have been laid out on pretty much the same plan — presumably that of the hill-forts they replaced.

The principal building was a rectangular church or oratory. Usually this would have been a timber-frame building with a thatched roof with either a filling of wattle and daub or a cladding of sawn planks, but on the west coast of Ireland and the northern isles of Scotland where gales sweep in from the Atlantic there are few trees and those that survive are stunted and bent double by the wind so that they look like a procession of very elderly people marching along the horizon. This is fortuitous for us because it means that in these areas the structures have survived because they were built using a traditional dry-stone (without mortar) walling technique familiar since the Bronze Age and still used in Britain today.

At Skellig Michael, eight miles off shore from Bolus Head in County Kerry, there are substantial remains preserved because of its almost inaccessible position and the absence of frost.

The monastic settlement is enclosed by stone walls, a necessary defence as we hear of monasteries raiding each other. Within the enclosure are two oratories of dry-stone construction. The monks' cells are dry-stone corbelled huts (*clochain* = beehive), a stone-built variant of the wattle and daub huts of parts of the mainland.

Perhaps a more likely model for the monastery on Cleenish Island is the one to be found on the island of Inishmurray, just four miles off the coast of Sligo and not too far from Lower Lough Erne. Here the enclosure wall survives in places to a height of 13 feet. Within the

Irish Beehive Hut

enclosure, which measures 175 feet x 135 feet, are the remains of oratories and monks' cells. Also preserved are several early decorated stones, some suggesting contact with the Eastern Church, the significance of which I will discuss in the next chapter. Other buildings that would be grouped around the oratories might be a refectory, a scriptorium, a school, a guest-house and an infirmary which would be added gradually as the community grew in size.

Aside from the usual rectangular timber-frame buildings there were two other building-styles to consider. At Kerry there is a boat-shaped oratory constructed of dry-stone walling. The use of up-turned boats to create basic sheds is not uncommon in British coastal areas and excavations from Trelleborg in Denmark present evidence of boat-shaped houses being used in a similar style within a fortified settlement, although it is unusual to find them reconstructed in stone.

Inland, where stone is harder to come by and timber was plentiful, instead of beehive huts the monks would more likely have chosen Celtic round-houses with wattle and

Kerry Oratory

daub walls and high thatched roofs. As Cleenish Island is a lake-island it is likely as it grew the area of settlement was augmented by a *crannog* — a village built on stilts extending the settlement over the lake. This was also true at Bangor where at least part of the monastic settlement extended into Strangford Lough.

What survives of these monastic buildings are only the foundations, and usually only those constructed of stone. Timber frames and thatched roofs don't survive in our damp northern climate for very many years and many important sites, which perhaps did originally boast stone buildings, have been built over by later generations.

Evidence of internal decoration has also disappeared. It may be that in their bid for austerity the monks eschewed ornamentation but there is no particular reason to suppose this. At St Albans Abbey wall paintings on plaster that survived from the 12th century (because they had been plastered over) give some idea as to how the early Christian churches may have been decorated. Their present condition (they faded drastically on contact with the air) explains why nothing has survived from the fifth and sixth centuries. Brightly coloured figurative images and elaborate decoration are still a feature of Greek Orthodox and other Eastern churches and these give us a glimpse of what the interiors of early Christian churches and chapels, and perhaps even the monks' cells looked like. Byzantine decorative arts were of a very high order and we know that the monks copied these designs in creating their illuminated manuscripts. It seems likely that they also copied them on their walls. The description of St Brigid's church in Kildare mentions paintings and hangings of linen (another speciality of the Byzantines although theirs were usually silk).

There seems no reason to suppose the monks lived in drab surroundings. Despite the austerity of their Rules their environment was colourful and pleasant. They had only to step outside to enjoy a magnificent view.

So until his middle teens Columbanus studied under Sinell. He would have received the usual "classical" education of the late Roman period studying Latin grammar, rhetoric, geometry and music and of course he would have extensively studied the Holy Scriptures as well as the tactics and use of arms required of every man qualified for military service.

The Irish, then as now, were particularly noted for their eloquence, as were all the Celts. In her book *The Celts* Nora Chadwick writes

> A number of Gaulish orators are known to us by name and the Romans were anxious to employ them as tutors to their sons. As late as the fourth century Symmachus, the greatest orator of his day, had been trained by a Gaulish rhetor (Chadwick, 1970, p. 46).

As late as the fourth century, she adds,

> … we are privileged to have an entrée into the great tradition of rhetorical training in the school of Bordeaux in the series of poems by Ausonius which celebrate the professors of rhetoric for several generations and trace their ancestry to the druids of Armorica (Brittany) (*Ibid.*).

For evidence that Columbanus was trained in this tradition and was particularly skilled in the subject of rhetoric we have only to look at his sermons of which no fewer than nineteen are extant.

It appears from Jonas's *Life* that he was not initially earmarked for a career in the church, but returned home after completing his education at Cleenish Island with a view to contemplating marriage. Then followed a disastrous love affair.

His monkish biographer assumes a damsel attempted to entice him into marriage, but being already committed to the prospect of a celibate life, Columbanus stoutly resisted her advances. He announced to his mother his intention of becoming a monk and so distressed her that she clung to him to prevent him crossing the threshold and he, we are told, rather heartlessly stepped over her (Jonas, p. 1).

This seems to contradict the previous story of his mother's conviction that he was predestined for the religious life. After the intensity of her vision she ought hardly to have been surprised.

Although many monks were seriously misogynist, Columbanus doesn't seem to have been one of their number. His later career reveals that he liked women and women liked him. It seems unlikely that his reaction to female interest was quite so prudish.

While it is possible that his final choice of career was prompted either by a failed love affair or the prospect of a distasteful arranged marriage (as a prince he would be expected to make a diplomatic match so this seems more likely), it's probable that a career in the church was the path his parents chose for him and his own intellectual inclinations took him to Bangor near Belfast where Comgall had established one of the most austere and learned of all the Irish monasteries. For the serious scholar this was the place to be.

Chapter 3

The Egyptian Influence

… this life should be considered as a road and an ascent …

Columbanus, Sermon V, "On Human Life" [1]

I have already employed the rather nebulous term "Christian Druidism" to define the specific brand of Christianity that characterised northern Europe and in particular the British Isles. Since the Druid religion had been around in some form or other for two, perhaps three thousand years before the arrival of Christianity it is reasonable to assume native beliefs had a considerable influence on early Christian ideas and observances. The influence on the dating of Christmas, for example, we know from Bede.

However it was not the only influence. People came to Britain from all over the Empire bringing their various sects with them. The most interesting immigrant influence from the point of view of the development of the Celtic Church in the sixth century — and perhaps the most surprising one — is that of the Egyptians.

Now you may think that to argue a connection between the British and Irish church in the far west and the heat of the Egyptian desert in the near east is a step into the realms of fantasy but this is not so. It is one of the most interesting and illuminating of connections and well worth a bit of exploration.

Columbanus went to Bangor, a huge monastery with — at its height, although probably not when he was there —

[1]   O'Fiaich, 1990, p. 90

around four thousand scholars, equivalent to a modern university. It was perhaps a sister-house to Bangor Iscoed with its two thousand four hundred scholars, twelve hundred of whom are reported to have died in the massacre during Columban's lifetime, although Bangor is simply the Celtic word for a monastery of the old-style, an enclosure surrounded by a wattle and daub fence (as a *crannog* would be). But the monastic tradition in the British Isles did not begin even with these substantial institutions, let alone the rather late arrival of Augustine of Canterbury.

Again let's refer back to those place-names — the remote rocky peninsulas and quiet groves, once the beloved haunt of druids, which now bear the names of obscure and barely remembered holy men and women.

The monastic tradition in the British Isles begins with hermits.

Although there was persecution in the British Isles prior to the sixth century it was patchy and sporadic, so in the absence of permanent opposition the Christians of the British Isles went in for a different form of martyrdom which the Irish perhaps inevitably called "Green Martyrdom" as opposed to the "Red Martyrdom" caused by the shedding of blood.

Green Martyrs were those who deliberately eschewed the comforts and pleasures of ordinary human society and retreated to some remote spot, a headland, an isolated beach (see St Govan's Head in South Wales for an example), to an island (see the many "Holy Islands" around Britain's coast) or to a mountain cave (see St Collen's retreat above Llangollen) to study the scriptures and devote themselves exclusively to prayer and, most importantly, the direct communion with God.

Hierarchy and Democracy in Religion and Society

There are two very important aspects to this communion with God which have shaped not just our religious thinking but our political philosophy as well down to the present day.

The first is that this is distinctly un-Roman. The Roman Catholic Church derived its shape and hierarchical structure from the imperial model and the system of patronage that is still found in Mediterranean societies today. No student of mafia movies can be unaware of the importance of the Godfather in that kind of hierarchical structure. Patronage is the route to success.

Authority is strictly regulated along pyramidal lines. To reach the summit the petitioner must progress up through each stage of the pyramid, seeking patronage from the next level of authority and then the next until eventually reaching the highest possible source of authority. Thomas Aquinas explained this hierarchy as a chain of being in which each individual knew his or her place. The worldly hierarchy is exactly mirrored in the pattern of the heavens.

Thus, in the Roman Catholic world view, which is the mirror image of a highly stratified social order, to reach God one must proceed as if approaching an emperor, through layers of functionaries supported and promoted by an influential patron. The chain of being is arranged in order of deference with man at the bottom. With the aid of a patron saint – or popularly the Virgin Mary – to act as intercessor the petitioner progresses up the chain through ranks of saints, apostles and angels to the throne of the ultimate patron, the Son of God, Christ, who acts as the final intercessor between the supplicant and God, the Father.

This is not as daft as it seems. All societies produce a cosmology that reflects the social structure on the ground. It provides a sort of mental map by which means the individual can locate his or her place in society. Roman Catholicism was reflecting a social structure that was at first imperial and then feudal. Authority was centralised and absolute and this is how it appears in the map of the heavens. It was for this reason as much as any other that until the late Middle Ages the cult of saints and of the Virgin Mary dominated Catholic religious practice.

Celtic society was also feudal but on a much smaller and more personal scale so attitudes to authority were very different. Even as late as the fourteenth century it was said a

Welshman (unlike an Englishman in Norman-French and Roman Catholic England) could always speak directly to his prince.

Thus our Celtic monks felt quite uninhibited about approaching God in a direct and personal manner. The hermits had initially no intermediary priests or litanies. They approached God through meditation and personal prayer. Only as they began to group together for security and companionship did a more complex approach to authority, both that of the church and the Almighty, arise.

This differing attitude to authority might seem trivial but it had serious political consequences of which we are currently the heirs. As societies change the mental map must also change to accommodate the changing circumstances of the individual. Paradoxically, as society becomes more complex, the cosmology that represents it is forced to become more simplified.

Once sub-cultures start to collide there is inevitable conflict of ideas. In order to avoid tensions arising between potentially hostile communities a mental map is sought which seeks out the universal. People begin to look for common ground that will allow them to co-exist comfortably as their economic and social circumstances dictate and their respective cosmologies begin to move from the particular to the general, from the group to the individual.

We can see this dynamic clearly at work in Ancient Greece. The Greek gods were arranged traditionally to reflect the political structure of the Mycenaean period. We know this because happily we have Homer recording events of fifteen hundred BC although written down in around the eighth century BC. On Olympus Zeus is the overlord just as Agamemnon in Homer is the High King. He dispenses justice and sees fair play when the lesser gods interfere in the affairs of men, just as the minor kings and nobles interfered in the affairs of their tenants and serfs.

By the fifth century Athens had changed. As the Greeks expanded their trading empire to take in the whole of the Mediterranean world they came into contact with other cosmologies and arrived at an inevitable point of conflict as these different ideologies started to collide with each other. Athenian society began to develop along cosmopolitan lines with a substantial merchant class. The model of kingship was no longer adequate. Something more flexible was needed. Something more representative of the different interests the city now contained. From kingship the Athenians gradually moved towards democracy.

In a monarchical state all decisions are left to the man (or woman) at the top. In a democratic state each citizen is required to think for him or herself and make their own decisions.

As the Athenians transformed themselves from subjects into citizens they made one other important change. They did not entirely abandon the religion of their forefathers but they began to question its validity. While respecting its traditional forms and social functions — the customs that defined their national identity and marked the rites of passage to which we all cling, rational or otherwise, as a sort of ethnic dress code — they developed a whole new intellectual framework. They invented philosophy.

Religion creates social cohesion instructing its celebrants in a specific moral code, providing them with a set of laws which they are required to obey and by this means conform to the wishes of the group and become social beings, which explains why the Athenians did not altogether abandon the traditional beliefs ingrained in their society.

Philosophy requires individuals to think for themselves. It requires a greater degree of self-consciousness, even self-absorption. One thing we can say of our early British and Irish hermits is that they were very self-absorbed.

Thomas Cahill suggests that the Irish discovered this self-awareness as a result of St Patrick's stories which he must have brought from mainland Britain, suggesting this was not a new idea there. We should in fact be very careful of Irish (or Celtic in general) claims to have "saved civilisation" since a brief consideration of developments in mainland Europe demonstrates that this was clearly not the case.

In 371 AD Martin (later St Martin) was elected Bishop of Tours where he held the episcopate for twenty-six years and we shall hear much from his successor Gregory later on. He lived at first as a recluse but later founded the monastery at Marmoutier near Tours which rapidly gained in great prestige.

Here we find the earliest model for the Columban monasteries. The enterprise was backed by the Romano-Gallic aristocracy and a number of the monks in the entourage of St Martin came from the best families in Gaul. Already we see the pattern that was later followed in Britain and Ireland.

In his own lifetime Martin not only established the episcopate at Tours, he created a vigorous community with a large number of monks.

Nora Chadwick notes

> The form of Christianity favoured by St Martin was monastic and to some extent eremitical. As he came from Bithynia[2] it was natural that this should be so, for it was the form of Christianity in vogue in the Egyptian desert and indeed throughout the East (1970, pp. 188–9).

And St Martin was not alone in introducing this Egyptian influence to Europe. Nora Chadwick goes on to describe how early in the fifth century the cenobotic life was introduced to the south of Gaul, first by the foundation of the monastery at Lerins by St Honoratus in the little group of islands off the Riviera and almost immediately afterwards by the foundation of a monastery near Marseilles by John Cassian. That of Cassian she points out was largely a contemplative institution and its founder had received his inspiration from his travels among the Desert Fathers in Egypt. His monastery, she adds, was a highly intellectual institution.

That there was a direct transfer of these models and ideals to Britain and Ireland is evidenced by the fact that St Patrick is said to have been a student at Lerins after his return from his period of slavery in Ireland in or around 410 AD. He did

---

[2]   Roughly modern Northern Turkey.

not return directly to Ireland but spent a long period living and studying in continental Europe before returning to Britain with the mission of St Germanus of Auxerre in 429AD. It was only then, on the death of the Bishop of Ireland Palladius, that he was able to fulfil his vocation to develop Christianity (which was self-evidently already there since they had a Bishop) in Ireland.

Columbanus, himself, made a point of visiting the shrine of St Martin at Tours (or attempting to because they would not let him in) when he found himself in the vicinity of the city, indicating that he was personally aware of the huge debt he owed to this founding father of European monasticism.

St Patrick's stories demonstrate the breadth of Christian influence which British Christians insisted came to their islands almost contemporaneously with the crucifixion of Jesus, since they cherished the legend that it had been brought to Britain by Joseph of Arimathea (and thus arrived slightly before the Romans).

If this is true then we can discount the theory that Christianity was simply the state religion imposed by the conquering Romans. So what was the appeal of Christianity to barely Romanized Britain in the early first century and even less Romanized Ireland in the sixth? What made Christianity more than an obscure Jewish sect?

Judaism, at least in its Old Testament form, was about man's place in society. In the Old Testament Jehovah is the God of the Israelites — the entire tribe — so that when one man sins the entire people suffers as a result. It's a completely social code.

Christianity, by contrast, is not primarily about an individual's place in society *per se*, but about an individual's position in relation to the whole of Creation. It's self-centred not in the sense that it is selfish, since morally it is designed to be quite the opposite, but in that it is centred on the self.

In this respect — in its use of meditation and mystical experience, its non-institutional and personal nature — in its original form it had much more in common with Hinduism and Buddhism than the temple-dominated "functional" and very public Graeco-Roman faiths or even the Judaism from which it borrowed its moral code.

This model seems to have sat comfortably with druidism, although annoyingly we know nothing at all about druid beliefs since they never wrote anything down. In the next chapter we will consider what is meant by Christian Druidism, but the impression one gets from the enthusiasm with which Christians in Britain and Northern Europe adopted this form of monasticism suggests that it was already in use; and the literary tradition of ancient wizards living in isolated towers, who were really scholarly hermits engaged in meditation and mysticism rather than purveyors of magic, rather confirms this view.

The model that they adopted was that of the Egyptian anchorites who, also lacking the opportunity to provide proofs of their faith by suffering under the yoke of physical persecution, had devised a new test of holiness by living alone and braving all sorts of physical deprivations and psychological terrors, imposing on themselves a near impossible asceticism by way of shedding the imposition of the body and achieving the transcendental state of pure spirit, the transfiguration reported in the Bible, the moment when the man Jesus momentarily and before our eyes becomes Christ.

The nearest modern equivalent to these spiritual adventurers are Hindu sadhus and given the historical timeframe the long arm of Hindu and Buddhist influence cannot be discounted although we can only trace the influence back with any certainty as far as Egypt.

The Egyptian connection was further strengthened in the years before Columbanus went to Bangor by the arrival of Coptic refugees. The Ulster monastery of Bangor in particular claimed in its litany to be *"ex Aegypto transducta"* (transferred from Egypt, or possibly "copied from the Egyptian").

One half of a 6th-century ivory diptych from
Constantinople (in the British Musuem).

The size of a small book, it is an example of the kind of
light portable item carried by Syrian refugees.

Artistic Links

As further evidence we can cite the habit of Coptic scholars of using red dots to adorn manuscript initials which is first glimpsed in Irish books from this time indicating that British and Irish monks on the very western fringe of the Roman Empire nevertheless had access to books from the cultured and scholarly East (Cahill, 1995, p. 180).

Nora Chadwick has studied the Celtic crosses of the valley of the Barrow, noting particularly the Moone Cross of Kildare, the Cross of Muiredach and the west Cross of Monasterboice, the Cross of the Scriptures at Clonmacnoise and the Cross of Durrow. She records

> It is particularly noticeable in this group of crosses that all the scenes are subordinated with great care to the representation of Christ, generally at the crossing or occupying the arms, whether it is Christ crucified or in glory, or as judge. The crucifixion is very stereotyped and generally bears the figures of the sponge and the lance-bearer below the arms of the crucified figure, an early arrangement of which is found on a page of the sixth-century Syrian Gospels of Rabula (1970, p. 244).

Popular subjects are scenes from the lives of saints, especially the meeting of Paul and Antony in the desert. Saint Antony appears to have been a favourite saint and role model.

In manuscript work this artistic style can be traced back to the time of Columbanus in the early manuscripts from Bobbio and in Ireland in the Book of Durrow (which may have been produced in Britain) which clearly demonstrates this decorative tradition. The red dots surrounding the initials are very characteristic of Coptic manuscripts of the Egyptian desert.

The opening page of the Gospel of St Mark in the Book of Durrow is entirely surrounded with red dots. There are few colours—a deep green, a bright yellow and a glowing red. These colours and much of the border design are used in the earliest surviving Coptic manuscripts and recall the manuscripts of the Eastern Mediterranean from Syria, Mesopotamia and Egypt.

Some of the frames of the Syrian Gospels of Rabula of the sixth century have pages of text with frames of interlacing very similar to those found in the Book of Durrow. Similar features are found in the Lindisfarne Gospels suggesting this influence was not confined to Irish monasteries. There is, therefore, a good deal of physical evidence to link the northern islands of Europe with Eastern scholarship.

Now this is a very, very interesting connection when we come to consider the kind of Christian influences that shaped not only Columbanus but his predecessors and successors from Finnian to Calvin, from Columcille to Martin Luther, for as well as shaping their artistic talent and physical organization it appears to have had a profound effect on their theology.

The Secret Book of John: **The Nature of God**

In 1945 at Nag Hammadi in Egypt the "Gnostic" gospels were discovered and among them "The Secret Book of John" which was not secret at all except in the sense that it had become unknown in the West after the early mediaeval period until this very modern discovery.

That the Irish and British knew this book or a version of it and had acquired copies from their Coptic brethren explains why their subsequent theology differs so diametrically from Roman orthodoxy.

In his book *Early Celtic Christianity* Brendan Lehane refers to "the Irish pursuit of apocryphal works condemned time and again by popes which nevertheless continued in favour in Irish schools". The south of Ireland he suggests had "taken its character from Spain and Aquitaine—the last Celtic refuges on the Continent—and indirectly from the eccentric churches of Syria and Egypt" (Lehane, 2005, p. 198).

That this connection was important in the life of Columbanus is confirmed by Jonas who mentions a specific friendship between Columbanus and a "Syrian woman" and makes it clear that they are allies (Jonas, p. 20).

The Venerable Bede, resident of the monastery of Wear-mouth, although paying lip-service to Roman orthodoxy, was clearly sympathetic to the Celtic cause. He relates at some length the debate at the synod of Whitby in which the Northumbrian King eventually came down in favour of the Roman party and notes that part of Colman's defence of the Irish position was that the Celtic church looked to St John as the source of its authority.

The Roman party on their side pointed out that their authority was derived from St Peter, who had founded the church in Rome, and it was on the basis that Jesus was said to have nominated Peter as his successor that Osbert, the King sitting in judgement, came down in favour of the Romans.

Colman was referring specifically to the matter of calcu-lating Easter but we may guess this Johannine source of authority applied more generally from the passionate delight the Celts took in Trinitarianism — the one thing above all that united them, despite many differences, with the Roman Catholics (Colgrave, 1999, p. 153).

For this reason it's instructive to look closely at this "secret book" and see what it contained that shaped our Irish monk and how he saw himself in relation to God.

The first part of the book outlines a philosophical theory that is clearly Platonic and Hellenic in origin, although it also approximates to the ideas put forward in the Wisdom of Solomon which suggests a fusion of Hebrew and Greek ideas.

More to the point it illuminates that most baffling of para-graphs that opens the Gospel of John, to which Anglican Christians listen attentively every Christmas at the popular service of the Nine Lessons and Carols, and, in most cases, fail to make head or tail of.

> In the beginning [intones the Vicar],was the Word, and the Word was with God and the Word was God. He was in the beginning with God. All things come into being through him, and without him not one thing came into being. What has come into being in him was life and the life was the light of all the people. The light shines in the darkness and the darkness did not overcome it (*John* 1.1–5).

You can sense in the service a big question-mark forming itself over the congregation as everyone thinks *"What?"*

The truth is, that without this second ("secret") book of John, containing an extended version of the theory that is outlined at the beginning of the Gospel of John, this passage doesn't really make any sense. The secret book is missing from the New Testament, yet it is absolutely central to understanding the ideas that drove Columbanus and his contemporaries.

John's theory is essentially as follows.

In the beginning there was not nothing because nothing by definition can't produce anything of substance. There was *something* (pretty much everyone is agreed on this *something*) which for the want of any better term he calls the Monad.

He calls it this because he likens it to a monarchy where there is a single authority at the apex of a pyramidal structure above which there can be nothing else.

In other words the Monad represents the highest possible authority. Beyond that we know nothing about it.

John writes

> ... it is not right to think of him as a god or something similar. For he is more than a god, since there is nothing above him, for no-one lords it over him ... He is not corporeal nor is he incorporeal. He is neither large, nor is he small. There is no way to say "What is his quality?" or "What is his quantity?" for no-one can know (Ehrman, 2003, p. 298).

In other words, when trying to account for the origins of the universe the answer is we can deduce there was a beginning but we can have no idea what that beginning consisted of.

In attempting to find a term to describe it John calls it the Logos which simply means "The Word". It's a word that has no meaning because we can attach no definition to it. We might call it "The Unknown."

In terms of modern astrophysics we might describe it as a combination of pure energy and matter/antimatter which physicists suggest collided in the "big bang" when the universe began. But neither the scientific nor the ancient description actually tells us how the universe got started, and certainly not why. John tries to answer the question by means of logical deduction following the method of Plato.

Man is a creative creature. By analysing the process of creation John attempts to work out how that process must have worked at the very beginning.

Creation needs two things to start with—energy and material of some sort. This is the starting-point—this is all we can say the Unknown—the Invisible Spirit of God—consists of. Beyond that we have no idea.

However energy and material in themselves do not lead to creation. Creation implies some sort of intention.

The human mind is constituted so that it constructs things according to a pattern and imposes order on them. We see the same sort of process at work in Nature where we identify similar patterns so it seems to us that this cannot be a random arrangement of things. For the creation of the universe to find its parallel in human creation there must have been some form of creative intelligence.

You will have noticed that John characterises the Prime Mover, as it is sometimes called, as male. This is not being simply sexist. The pattern of reproduction in human terms requires two parties, male and female. From the Prime Mover, the male principle, we therefore have to move to the female principle.

This is Sophia. John makes it clear we are still in the realm of the abstract. Sophia is not a personification but a Spirit with five characteristics—the Pentad.

These five characteristics are *thought, foreknowledge, indestructibility, eternal life* and *truth.* All five are combined in the one word, Wisdom.

To move further along the evolutionary path male and female have to be combined. The Logos combined with Wisdom produces the third element necessary to begin creation.

First you need to generate power and some sort of material to create something from, next you need the creative intelligence to decide to do something with it and then lastly you need a deed—the act of creation itself. This third element is identified as Christ — the Christ Pantocrator of the Byzantines — Christ the Creator of the Universe . This is not the man Jesus who is later identified as the human embodiment of Christ. This is the Lord of the Dance, the Spirit of Life.

For creation to take place then you need three things — will (*Logos*), thought (*Sophia*) and life (*Christ*). These three together form the basis of the Christian Trinity. These are not three gods, which is a common misconception, but three attributes that go together to make up the indivisible whole which is what we understand by the word God.

For convenience John identifies them in human terms as Father, Mother and Son — the pattern of the Holy Family. He also refers to the Trinity as the Autogenes — the thing that can create of itself literally. You might compare it to an amoeba which can reproduce itself except that an amoeba can only produce another amoeba. The Autogenes/God can create whatever it wants at will because it has within its compass energy, matter and will, wisdom and the ability to create life. In this respect we can say that God made man in his own image since, within the limitations of our own capacity for invention, this is also true of human beings.

There is nothing unscientific in this thinking. Scientists are busy looking for the building blocks of creation — nanotechnology and gene research are all trying to get back to that original material. What are we made out of? Every step we take we find out how little we actually know. An even more difficult question to answer is why?

Because it's difficult to explain even philosophical concepts solely in abstract terms the image of the Holy Family is used as a way of illustrating the process of creation and in the Christian era, this Holy Family became identified with the human family of Jesus. (Here at once we encounter a gap between the philosophical use of imagery and historical accuracy. One apocryphal book suggests that Jesus was in fact one of twins which means in the scene of the Nativity there should be two babies in the manger but traditionally there is only ever one.)

The Father is still acknowledged to be God, with Joseph standing in as substitute, but the Mother of God — the Theotokos — properly speaking the "sacred feminine" Sophia becomes inextricably linked with the Blessed Virgin Mary, the earthly mother of Jesus.

It was perhaps for this reason rather than out of misogyny that the early fathers of the church at the Council of Nicaea altered the creed from John's Father-Mother-Son to "Father, Son and Holy Spirit" (or Holy Ghost which means the same thing) to avoid the suggestion that worship of the Trinity permitted the sort of idolatrous worship of the Mother Goddess that was common amongst the pagans.

Thus far John has given us the very earliest origins of the universe which I will represent in tabular form as follows.

Will	The Unknown (Logos)
	The invisible spirit of which we know nothing — We can only logically deduce by working backwards that it exists
Thought	**Wisdom (Sophia)**
	Consisting of five elements
	Thought
	Foreknowledge
	Eternal Life
	Indestructibility
	Truth
Life	**Christ Pantocrator**
	The Spirit of Life — Creator of the Universe

These three comprise the Holy Trinity that we understand by the word God.

The Secret Book of John: **Human Fulfillment**

John further analyses the make-up of Christ by suggesting he presides over four stages or aeons under which John groups the different elements of personality that make up the perfect man.

			Perfection
			Peace
			Wisdom
		Understanding	
		Love	
		Imagination	
	Conception		
	Perception		
	Memory		
Grace			
Truth			
Form			

The teachings of Jesus relate directly to this intellectual construct. Jesus is the human embodiment of Christ because he is the perfect man who has reached stage four, the highest state of perfection a man can reach while still in the body — rather as in Buddhism the Buddha is the man who has reached a similar stage of perfection.

The objective of his teaching is to help other individuals to raise themselves through these stages. By the time they have reached the fourth stage the human soul is beginning to approach a similar form to the Trinity. After death therefore it may be absorbed into it just as the Buddhist on becoming Buddha achieves Nirvana.

Most early lives of saints end with the saint on his or her deathbed being received into the light. A classic description can be found also in Malory where Galahad, the perfect virgin knight, reaches the Holy Grail.

In the moment he dies his soul is received into heaven by three "angels" representing the Trinity. The Holy Grail it turns out is not a cup or any physical artefact but enlightenment. It is the end of the road.

The first two stages, the physical form and cognitive abilities might be said to be acquired at birth but the next stage requires socialisation and education and the qualities necessary for this, understanding, love and the ability to have ideas and develop a vision of the world require teaching, and much of the teaching of Jesus is designed to enable his disciples to acquire these gifts.

Before we get too hung up on the idea that Christianity is essentially misogynist I should point out that John describes the Trinity in its entirety as the "thrice-named androgynous One" stressing that the Male-Female-Child subdivisions are only analogous and not intended to suggest that God is either a "he" or a "she".

This explains the Byzantine acceptance of a "third sex", the presence of a considerable number of eunuchs in their society — not as slaves but as individuals making a significant contribution — and, in the context of the monastic tradition in both East and West, the high value placed on celibacy, for achieving sexlessness is another way of drawing closer to the condition of God. Thus Galahad, in his "virgin" condition, is able to reach the Holy Grail whereas his father Lancelot, who famously was involved in an adulterous affair which he is unable to give up, is allowed only to glimpse the Grail but not approach it. He has fallen short of the standard of perfection required.

Unfortunately in seeking to emphasise this androgynous nature by converting the feminine Sophia into the Holy Spirit the early fathers of the church unbalanced the nature of the Trinity heavily in favour of the male, an imbalance still perpetuated in the Roman Catholic Church and until very recently the Church of England.

Another argument for supposing that our Celtic Christians had read this supposedly "secret" book of John and were well versed in the philosophy within its pages lies in the fact that women were accorded equal status within the Celtic Church. Monasteries were open to both sexes and women, like Hild of Whitby and Brigid of Kildare, women of the highest rank, presided over a "double house" of both men and women and were powerful Abbesses in their own right.

Excavations in 1977 at Amay in Belgium have produced evidence that there were women bishops within the Celtic Church. Columbanus always had a bishop with him and there were complaints of unspecified Abbots travelling with women so perhaps at times this bishop was a woman since it's likely that the criticisms were aimed at him.

The native societies throughout Northern Europe were perfectly accustomed to strong-minded women who competed with men on more or less equal terms as we shall see when we meet the formidable Frankish queens.

Indeed the Celtic Church positively encouraged intimate relations between the sexes of a non-physical nature.

Another custom officially banned by the Council of Nicaea in the early fourth century was the practice of spiritual marriage between monks and nuns and the acquisition of a "soul-friend". St Comgall, Columbanus' mentor at Bangor, even recommended it. "A man without a soul friend", he said, "is like a body without a head". (And what woman would argue with that?)

The need for a soul-friend was connected to another cause of dispute between the churches. In the Roman church the practice of confession was a public affair — the shaming of a sinner by appearing at the church door in sackcloth and ashes made this a useful method of social control.

Within the Celtic Church confession was a private matter, a cleansing of the self — we are back again to this dichotomy between society and the self. A soul-friend was someone you could confess to in absolute confidentiality. The notion of the secrecy of the confessional originates here. Also the Irish secular clergy were allowed to marry — another link with the practices of the East.

Greek Orthodox priests have always been allowed — indeed encouraged — to be married men.

It's easy to see why this Egyptian influence had a profound effect on the Irish and British who peculiarly and naturally combined a taste for mysticism with vigorous rationalism. It's no surprise that they warmed to the ideas of Christianity which is fundamentally rationalist in its arguments but mystical in its practice.

Columbanus later wrote to the Pope in defence of his fellow Celts "Liberty was the tradition of my fathers and among us in Ireland no person prevails but rather reason."

In his thinking we can see the ardent rationalist analysing Nature as the window through which we can glimpse the workings of the Creator. Nature, he says, is a second revelation to be read alongside the Scriptures to deepen our knowledge of God.

> Who then is God? [he asked]. He is Father, Son and Holy Spirit, yet one God. Seek no further concerning God, for those who wish to know the great deep must first study the nature of things. Knowledge of the Trinity is properly compared to the depth of the Sea... If a man therefore wishes to know the deepest ocean of divine understanding, let him first, if he is able, scan that visible sea. The less he finds his knowledge to be of those creatures which lurk beneath the sea, the more he should realise his ignorance of the depths of his Creator... Why, I ask, does a man who doesn't know earthly things propound on the heavenly? (Columbanus, Sermon "On Faith").

This brand of Christianity is not therefore anti-scientific, since it's through empirical observation that we can understand how God is made manifest in the universe.

The Celtic Christians did not burn books, they cherished all forms of intellectual endeavour, Christian and pagan, and did as much to preserve and protect the knowledge of the classical world as that of the church fathers.

In his day to day life, his penitential rule, we see the pilgrim progressing through John's four stages of human growth, attempting to reduce the dependence on worldly things in order to refine the spirit and make it fit to achieve transcendence to the point where man becomes Christ.

It must have been with John's analysis of the idea of God in mind that he wrote:

> God is everywhere, utterly vast and everywhere near at hand, according to his own witness of himself. "I am", he says, "a God at hand and not a God afar off". The God we are seeking is not one who dwells far away from us, we have him within us, if we are worthy. For he resides in us like soul and body, if only we represent him as we should, if we are not dead to him in sin. Who, I say, can explore the

highest summit of this unutterable and immeasurable being? Who can examine the secret depths of God? Who will dare to think they can put their finger on the eternal source of the universe? Who dares boast that they know the mind of God who is infinite and unknowable, who fills all and surrounds all and passes beyond all, who occupies all and transcends all, whom no-one has ever seen as he is? Therefore, let no-one think he can seek out the unsearchable aspects of God, the nature, mode and cause of his existence. They are indescribable, undiscoverable, unsearchable. Only believe in simplicity and yet with firmness that God is and shall ever be as he has been for God is unchanging.[3]

This is Columbanus influenced by the neo-Platonic philosophy of the "Syrians". But that was not the only influence from outside Roman orthodoxy.

In the next chapter we must consider the influence of the Druids. I have mentioned "Christian Druidism" in connection with the Celtic Church but to understand how this influenced Columban's thinking we need to examine exactly what this means.

---

[3]   From "Sermon on Faith" in *Columbanus: Studies on the Latin Writings*, ed. Michael Lapidge (Boydell Press, 1997).

Chapter 4

Christian Druidism

Now we hear the echo of another influential Welshman, St Patrick, whose creed differs significantly from the Apostles' Creed favoured by the Roman church (and the Church of England) and echoes perhaps a faint chorus of those mysterious druids who saw God in every aspect of the natural world. St Patrick's creed has an altogether more universal outlook.

> Our God, God of all men,
> God of heaven and earth, seas and rivers,
> God of sun and moon, of all the stars,
> God of high mountains and lowly valleys,
> God over heaven and in heaven and under heaven,
> He has a dwelling
> In heaven and earth and sea
> And in all things that are in them.
> He gives a being to all things,
> He gives life to all things.
> He is lord over all things,
> He nurtures all things.
> He makes the light of the sun to shine.
> He surrounds the moon and stars.
> He has made wells in the arid earth
> And placed islands in the sea
> And stars to give light to the planets.
> He has a son co-eternal with himself
> Like himself.
> The Son is not junior to the Father
> Nor the Father senior to the Son
> And the Holy Spirit breathes in them.
> They are not separate beings,
> Father and Son and Holy Spirit (Brown, 2006, p. 70).

No mention of the "holy catholic church", no suggestion of subjection to any higher authority other than that of God and, by appealing to the "God of all men" making a virtue of toleration and underlining the notion that before the supreme authority we are all equal.

Patrick was born in 393 AD[1] and spent his early years as a slave having been captured by pirates. He returned to Britain around 410 AD — the year in which the Roman Empire's hold on Britain finally and irrecoverably collapsed. After a short spell back in Britain he decided to pursue the religious calling that had come to him during his years of slavery and set off to the continent to further his studies.

He seems to have gone first to Lerins in the south of Gaul and then to Auxerre where he was a contemporary of St Germanus. It is likely that he was back in Britain with St Germanus, who was on a preaching tour in 432 AD when they heard the news that the Bishop of Ireland, Palladius, had died. Patrick was appointed Bishop of Ireland in his place and the rest as they say is history.

It appears that Patrick was not the first to convert the Irish to Christianity but he was certainly the most effective in making Christianity the dominant religion and it was his brand of Christianity that Columbanus inherited so it's worth taking a moment to consider how that brand was created.

It is often said that the druids left no scriptures as their ideas were so esoteric (by which we understand "off the wall") that they were kept secret by a priesthood popularly characterised by sorcery and human sacrifice.

Druidism goes back a long way and at an early stage, as with most of the world's religions, shamanism and sacrifice — even *in extremis* human sacrifice — undoubtedly played their part. Our most abiding image of druidism comes from Julius Caeser, whose descriptions of his opponents in the Gallic Wars are truly terrifying — as he

---

[1] There is considerable disagreement about the year of Patrick's birth but the general concensus seems to be that it was around 390AD. 393AD seems a reasonable assumption working backwards from the date of his return to Britain and subsequent career.

intended them to be— but this was fifty years before the birth of Jesus. By 410 AD, more than four centuries down the line, mainstream druidism seems to have taken on a very different character.

Sacrifice—human or animal—had been outlawed a century earlier when Rome officially adopted Christianity as the religion of the state. It is impossible that four hundred years of classical influence and state interference had not had its effect on the native religion.

Druidism, like all mainstream religions, contained a moral code and a set of ideas and yes we do know what they were.

In the late fifth century a Celtic monk—we do not know his name—wrote a book called *The Wonderful History of the Sword in the Stone.* The original of this book does not exist but most of it is to be found in Thomas Malory's *Mort d'Arthur* and was published in English by William Caxton in the late fourteenth century after Malory, so he tells us, found the manuscript in a chest in the library of Salisbury Cathedral.

Its importance to the British is perhaps reflected in the fact that after the Bible it was the next book Caxton chose to print although it is a huge tome which at the time would have been very expensive to produce.

Malory's version of the text is somewhat jumbled indicating the state the manuscript was in when he found it. Different parts of the book are printed in different places in the *Mort d'Arthur* interspersed with mediaeval romances of the 11th and 12th centuries and earlier chronicles produced a century or so after the "Sword" book which relate the history of the real King Arthur who died in 543 AD.

The *Sword in the Stone* was written towards the end of the fifth century and so does not refer to the real King Arthur at all but a mythical role model. It does not give us history as an historian would understand it, although it does give us one or two useful dates. It is not a chronicle but an ideological history telling us in terms of cosmology how Christian Druidism came into being.

As an illustration of the gradual transition of Druidism to Christianity in the fifth century and the continuity of ideas here are two versions of the same prayer.

The first is taken from the Great Book of Margam and is a traditional ancient Welsh prayer handed down by the "gwyddoniaid" the "wise men" and seems to express Druid belief before the merger with Christianity with its emphasis on the equation of light and truth—"gwynvyd"—the world of white (heaven) and God.

The second is credited to St Talharain, a fifth century Celtic Christian saint and has been slightly modified to give us a neat picture of how these principles have been adapted to match Celtic Christian ideals with the emphasis now on reason and knowledge as the way to truth.Both prayers retain a sense of everything in Nature—the worldly and the otherworldly—being connected. St Talharain's inclusion of social justice as one of the steps to achieving perfection suggests he (or she) was influenced by Pelagius.

From the Great Book of Margam

God impart to me thy strength
And in that strength endurance
And the ability to bear everything for the truth
That in the truth I may see the light
And in that light the world of white
A glimpse of heaven
And in that glimpse of heaven come to know love
And in that love come to know God
And in God, everything that is good.

St Talharain's Prayer (5th century)

God impart to me thy strength
And in that strength, reason;
And in reason, knowledge,
And in knowledge, justice
And in justice the love of it;
And in the love of justice, the love of everything
And in the love of everything
The love of God.

Christian Druidism was formed by a merger between the early Christian British church and the mainstream Druid church. We are given a date for this event—the feast of Pentecost 454 AD, the date on which the quest for the Holy Grail begins, but it is clear from Patrick's own account of his mission that there had been a gradual process of assimilation going on during the preceding fifty years.

The book is immensely valuable not just because it is the first true British novel (although presumably not originally written in English but in Latin). It is an account of the development of the religious life in Britain.[2]

The first part of the story introduces us to a wholly Celtic cosmology and explains how the Sword of Truth and the Spear of Justice were forged and given to Man by the Gods.

In the second part of the story Britain begins to undergo changes as Saxons and Romans alter the religious landscape. By the time we get to the famous story "The Sword in the Stone" Christians and Druids are operating side by side and sharing the same buildings—in that particular story Westminster Abbey, which seems to have been a temple to Merlin as he presides there, sharing it with the Archbishop of Canterbury. This is very interesting as this reflects a deliberate policy by the Christians to achieve a rapprochement with their pagan counterparts. Later on we will find Columbanus using this method to great effect in his own missionary work.

By the middle of the fifth century this rapprochement has reached a point where the two religions are ready to merge and Britain becomes wholly Christian. In the *Quest for the Holy Grail* the Christian communion chalice is merged with the Druid cauldron of inspiration and immortality (both believed to mystically contain the Holy Spirit) to produce what amounts to a corporate logo. At around the same time the Chi-Ro symbol acquires its surrounding circle.

---

[2]   There are definitely no wizards in the book. Sorcery is strongly disapproved of and it is made quite clear that any such residual elements in druidism are among those left behind. Gods associated with magic are the ones that do not make the cut into the Christian era.

Chi-Rho symbol from a 4th-century mosaic floor at Woodchester. The symbol is surrounded by a wreath, an early suggestion of a mixed Christian/Pagan household.

In the Quest story the Gods of the Celtic Pantheon set out to achieve enlightenment and learn the secrets of Christian mysticism. It is Galahad, the last of the sky-gods and the first of the Christian knights, who finally achieves this transition. The author of the book with perfect sincerity is able to liken Galahad — the perfect knight — to Jesus Christ. Here is a point of contact between the two religions.

The reason I spent some time in the previous chapter outlining the analysis of the Trinity in the *Secret Book of John* was to stress its importance to both religions. This was the other principal point of contact. Patrick famously used the leaf of the shamrock to explain the Trinity to the Druids but they already had a Trinity of their own so they could not have found the idea totally alien.

Although the Celts had many local gods and spirits of place above them all was the Creator God, Mathonwy, whose name means "The Greatest Treasure of All". Mathonwy has three children — his daughter Don (Dana to the Irish), who together with her husband Beli express the idea of Life and Death. It is Beli who owns the Sword of

Carol of the Rose

There is no rose of such virtue
As is the rose that bare Jesu;
                 Alleluia.

For in this rose contained was
Heaven and earth in little space;
                 Res miranda.

By that rose we may well see
That he is God in persons three,
                 Pares forma.

The angels sungen the shepherds to:
Gloria in excelsis deo:
                 Gaudeamus.

Leave we all this worldly mirth,
And follow we this joyful birth;
                 Transeamus.

Alleluia, res miranda,
Pares forma, gaudeamus,
                 Transeamus.

This little carol neatly expresses the complex philosophy of the idea of the Trinity—all living things being the work of the Creator God who is observed in Nature.

The song is at least 500 years old and may be descended from a much older Latin version. At all events it is evidence of a revival of Celtic Christianity at the time of the reformation.

Truth and acts as judge to decide who is and who is not guilty of sin. These two together comprise the Celtic equivalent of Christ both as the Spirit of Life and the Judge in the Afterlife.

Don has two brothers. One is Math or Merlin, the god of wisdom who corresponds to Sophia or the Holy Spirit. He is not a magician but enters the Sword story whenever the gods (for none of them are really human — the whole of the action takes place in the Otherworld) need information or guidance. As the narrative moves from the pagan to the Christian era Merlin is replaced by a whole series of Celtic monks who perform the same function within a Christian context.

Her other brother is Lir, God of the Sea, which to people who lived on the edge of the Atlantic Ocean and had no idea what, if anything, might be on the other side, represented the Unknown — John's Logos.

It was this intellectual framework that allowed the Druids to merge with the Christians. Fundamentally at an abstract level their theology was the same. As a result we find that the Celtic Christians from Patrick onwards are passionate Trinitarians. At times their devotion to the Trinity and the Creator God seems to override more overtly Christian theology.

Not all the druids of course were of the same intellectual bent and Druidism continued to operate in the British Isles at least until the latter end of the sixth century when Columba (Columcille) took his mission to the Picts but the merger seems to have been accepted at least throughout what is now England and Wales as we don't hear anything further of the Druids after the mid-fifth century. The only religious battles recorded are between the two branches of the Christian church and the pagan beliefs of the immigrant Saxon and Vikings.

One aspect of the book we should mention in passing is its decidedly anti-Roman stance.

In the Quest story all the abbeys are White Abbeys — that is to say they are Abbeys within the Celtic Church. The only time we encounter a black-robed Roman priest he turns out to be an agent of the devil, which gives some sort of clue as to the writer's feelings towards the Roman church.

Another aspect of the book which is important is the great trouble the author takes to demonstrate that the Celtic Church has developed independently of the Roman Empire.

Generally it would be said that Christianity came to Britain with the Romans but the White Monks are adamant that it arrived directly from the Holy Land brought by Joseph of Arimathea, uncle of Jesus (hence he is also represented as having brought the Holy Grail).

The first date we are given in the book is 40AD. The story told is wholly Celtic but the date on which Nisien (the Celtic God of Peace) wins the Sword of Truth for the Kings of Britain is significant as this would coincide with the date of the Pauline missions. The Epistles of Paul indicate that by the mid first century there were already Christian communities spread throughout the Mediterranean. The implication of this story is that the Kings of Britain first embraced Christianity in 40 AD or thereabouts which could of course be true. If so, the claims of the Celtic Church were justified. Christianity had arrived in Britain prior to the Romans who did not begin to arrive in numbers until after the Claudian invasion of 43 AD.

The significance of the legend, true or not, is that it established that the Celtic Church in Britain was entirely independent of Rome.

The direct link with Jesus also gave rise to the idea that the British version of Christianity (and later also the Irish and Scottish) was somehow a "pure faith" unsullied by Roman politics.

In introducing his *Life of Columbanus* the monk Jonas makes this point. His first words are

> Columban, who is also called Columba, was born on the island of Ireland. This is situated in the farthest ocean and is said to be charming. Here live the Scots who, although they do not live under Roman law, flourish in the strength of Christian doctrine to which they are more faithful than all of their neighbours.
>
> Columban was born when that island's faith was in its

infancy in order that the religion which that race cherished uncompromisingly might be increased by his own fruitful labours and nurtured by his associates (Jonas, p. 1).

We will see how Columbanus was influenced by this idea in his correspondence with the various Popes and Bishops he locked horns with in his career. He did not believe he was in any way bound to obedience to Rome.

We do not know who wrote the Quest book but we do know something about its importance to the history of British Christianity.

There is a legend — which is probably not a legend but has some basis in fact — that Illtud and Cadoc were the "keepers of the Grail."

This is probably not a legend because Illtud and Cadoc were real people and pivotal to the development of Celtic Christianity in the early sixth century.

It is highly unlikely that they were the keepers of the legendary chalice, although that has not stopped generations of treasure-seekers hoping that they were. It is made quite clear at the end of the book that the Grail does not exist in the material world.

At the end of the story the author tells us

> … the two friends saw a heavenly hand — just the hand not the body — reach down and take the Holy Grail containing the Holy Spirit. It picked up the Spear of Justice and the Sword of Truth and then it vanished, returning them to the place from which they had come.
>
> Since then no man has ever been so foolish as to claim that he had seen the Holy Grail (my translation; see also Malory, 1996, p. 672).

The Holy Grail is a spiritual symbol. It can only be found by pursuing the religious life. That is the lesson of the book. But although Illtud and Cadoc could not have been the keepers of the Grail itself they could very well have been the keepers of the book, a treasure in itself and from what we know about them this is very likely.

Illtud was born in the late fifth century and was therefore too young to be the author but in 500 AD or thereabouts he set up the monastery at Llantwit Major in South

Glamorgan.[3] Within a short space of time Illtud's monastery had established a great reputation for scholarship which implies of course that they had an extensive library. Among the treasures of that library it seems was *The Wonderful History of the Sword in the Stone*. From here its ideals of Justice, Freedom, Truth, Equality, Hospitality and Chivalry (transmogrified into the Christian ideals of Charity and consideration for others) were carried far afield by the roll-call of great names of the mid-sixth century produced by what has been described as Britain's first university — Gildas, Paul Aurelian, Samson of Dol and many others. According to John Davies "almost all the leaders of early Irish monasticism had been trained in Wales" (Davies, 2007, p. 71).

I have already pointed out that these Irish and British monasteries found their models at Lerins and Tours where Egyptian influences were all the rage but they also had a native model of very long-standing.

According to Julius Caesar the Druids originated in Britain where the most famous of their schools of religious discipline were to be found and to which Celts from other countries came for training. They were natural philosophers (which in the modern era we call scientists) and noted for their scientific approach to healing — in the Quest story whenever we meet a druid he is usually a doctor. To be a druid priest required twenty years of training — a habit that seems to have been continued in the monastic schools as most of the early Celtic saints seem to have embarked on their missions relatively late in life.

The "Sword" book is very useful, as well as being a wonderful literary work, in that it gives us an indication of the intellectual life of Druidism as it informed the scholars of the Celtic Church.

---

[3] Properly speaking Llanilltud Fawr "The Great Church of Illtud" — Llan has roughly the same meaning as Bangor — a church community within an enclosure — which is why you find place-names beginning with Llan all over Wales indicating the spread of monastic establishments.

Aside from the very specific documentary evidence provided by the text in Malory there is some slight archaeological evidence to confirm the date of the merger.

During the Roman period and until the early seventh century British Christians did not use the familiar symbol of the Celtic cross. All the crosses are of a later date. Instead they used the Chi-Ro symbol. Where this symbol is found prior to the end of the fourth century it is normally found without a surrounding circle. An example of this can be found in the mosaic at the Roman villa at Hinton St Mary.

By the late fifth century we begin to find slab crosses inscribed with the Chi-Ro symbol inside a surrounding circle — another merged corporate logo combining the sun-circle of the Druids with the Chi-Ro symbol of the Christians. These slab crosses were gradually replaced by the familiar Celtic Cross where the sun circle appears within the arms of the cross or at the crossing.

This change of design is not definitive but it does suggest that the date of 454 AD given in Malory is accurate.

You may wonder why the Druids and Christians would wish to merge. The answer to that question is to be found in the history of the late fourth century. Nora Chadwick tells us:

> In Gaul Gratian initiated a series of measures which, in fact, banished paganism from the state, and his policy survived him. In 388 Arcadius in the East had the heathen temples destroyed, and Honorius in the West confiscated the temple revenues. In the fifth century paganism was deprived of all its rights. Deprived of sanctuaries and resources, and finally of its clergy it gradually gave way to Christianity (Chadwick, 1970, p. 190).

From the Druid point of view a merger with the Christians in Britain, Armorica and Gaul would have had the distinct advantage of giving its adherents state protection. The Christians, having themselves been proscribed throughout the Empire prior to 310 AD, no doubt felt a degree of empathy with their fellow-religionists.

Gratian's proscription however ceased to run after the Roman withdrawal in 410 AD and the situation was reversed. In the latter part of the fourth century AD, as the Roman hold on Britain was weakening there is evidence of a Celtic revival (*ibid.*, p. 165).

The "Sword" book very clearly reflects this burgeoning sense of nationalism. It is at this point that the "British" become an identifiable nation — no longer an agglomeration of ethnic groups organized on tribal lines and no longer entirely, although probably still predominantly, Celtic.

For the largely Romano-British Christians identifying themselves with the native tradition must have seemed like a good idea, gradually stripping themselves of the taint of association with the detested conquerors while retaining the civilised aspects of classical culture and scholarship which the Druids admired and respected. Seeking to establish their roots in a non-Roman source would have been part of this.

That the boot was now on the other foot is illustrated by what Marjorie Filbee tells us of the church organisation in Cornwall.

> The local saints did not try to change the monastic and sometimes solitary aspect of the early Celts. They managed to adapt their Christianity to the ways of the Celts, ensuring a peaceful transition in their religious practices. All this displeased the Church in Rome, which sometimes claimed that Cornish Christianity was simply a continuation of Druidism (Filbee, 1996, pp. 50–1).

So it was that Columbanus was imbued with two very un-Roman influences, but we should not lose sight of the fact that although the Britons had an antipathy to Roman government they were not averse to Roman culture.

The standard education for a boy entering a monastery until the late middle ages was modelled on that of a young Roman gentleman and Columbanus was as well versed in the classics as any man of his age.

His letters are filled with classical references. He includes Christian authorities like Jerome and Eusebius as you would expect but also imitations of Sappho, Horace, Ovid, Juvenal and Martial indicating the breadth of his reading and his preferred literary language was always Latin.

All of these influences had made their mark on the man who sailed away from the Irish coast.

Which brings us to our next question.

Why did he leave?

Chapter 5

Why did Columbanus leave Ireland?

Hatred kills a man's peace, love kills his integrity.

Columbanus, Letter to the Monks of Luxeuil, 610 AD[1]

When Columbanus wrote the above was it just a popular aphorism, a convenient text upon which to hang a sermon, or was he writing from his own experience? If so it suggests a man of more complex motives than his biographer would have us believe.

Jonas of Susa tells us that Columbanus simply asked permission of his abbot Comgall to go on what was later known as the greater peregrinatio — the further pilgrimage, that is to say he asked permission to permanently leave his native land making a vow never to return.

Jonas gives us no indication as to why he chose to make such a request and leaves us to imagine it was simply prompted by purely evangelical desires. This simple explanation seems a little disingenuous given the psychological complexity of the man and on a little further examination we can find plenty of other motives for his departure and to some of them Columbanus' later assertion that "Hatred kills a man's peace; love kills his integrity" may well hold the key.

He, above all, Thomas Cahill points out, affirmed the great Gospel virtue over all else: *Amor non tenet ordinem* — Love has nothing to do with order (Cahill, 1995).

---

[1]   Lehane, 2005, p. 171.

To Columbanus it appears love was a necessary but rather a messy business and certainly, as we shall see as we follow him through his later life, experience certainly proved that to be true.

There is a long-standing tradition in Ireland of the *peregrination* – the pilgrimage in which Irish monks took to the sea in a curragh, a boat of hides stretched over a timber frame – without mast or sail and entrusted themselves to God's mercy, in effect going wherever the currents carried them. This was later known as the "White Martyrdom". Generally, this alone, is held to be the explanation for Columbanus' unexpected departure.

However, there is reason to suppose that such a departure was not necessarily voluntary. Forcible exile in a boat without sail or oars was also a long-standing civil punishment. This would be a very severe punishment. The punishment for murder (or perhaps more accurately manslaughter) for a monk was ten years exile, existing for the first three years on bread and water (Brown, 2006, p. 106).

In the case of the monks later biographers enhanced the penitential aspects of their voyages with mystical allure. The voyage of St Brendan, at least that part of it which was not lifted from the earlier Celtic cosmology, perhaps records such a voyage endowing it with a mystical and religious significance, even the possibility that it was a scientific endeavour rather than a penitential one.

Columbanus could have met Brendan who didn't die until 577 AD by which time Columban was in his midthirties and he may have been inspired by him. However, Columbanus did not sail into the wide blue yonder or embark on a mystical voyage of discovery – he went to territory that was well-known and heavy with maritime traffic.

We have already considered that the tale Jonas tells us of how Columbanus became a monk falls some way short of the probable actuality. If it was a scandalous affair that drew him into the sanctuary of the monastic life that would explain the second half of his epigram.

For an explanation of the first half we can look at the career path of his namesake, the other Columba, whose proper name was Columcille.

Columcille, we are told, was so named in his early teens by a schoolmaster impressed with his scholarly virtuosity. It means "Colum of the Church" indicating the career path he was expected to follow.

Why then is he known to us as "Columba of Iona"? Who changed his name and why? His name was first changed, as was the norm, when he entered a monastery. Although we do not know the proper name of our Columbanus we do know the real name of Columcille.

His name was Crimthann, meaning "The Fox" which suggests he was "Red Irish", a red-haired Celt, and he was the younger son of a royal family, the cened-Conaill branch of the northern Ui Neill — in common parlance he was an O'Neill, the family that ruled Ulster until the seventeenth century conquest of the province by William of Orange (Cahill, 1995, p. 169).

He went into exile in Dalriada — western Scotland — in 563 AD following his judicial condemnation at the synod of Teiltu. He founded the monastery on Iona two years later in 565 AD and it is worth comparing this period with the time it must have taken Columbanus to set up his own foundations, as it will help us establish a time-frame for his arrival in France (Brown, 2006, pp. 106–7).

The story is that Columba's excommunication came about as a result of his taking part in a battle between the O'Neills and the High King Diarmid (Dermot) of Tara. This arose because Diarmid killed one of his followers, Curnan, who was a cousin and therefore a kinsman and Columcille was bound by the customs of the age to avenge his death. Curnan had apparently killed another young man during a hurling game triggering the blood feud and Columcille had given him sanctuary. For this reason Diarmid imprisoned Columcille. How had he broken out of prison? Had he killed the guard?

It might seem a rather unchristian way to proceed but Columcille was a member of a society which was bound together by a web of kinship obligations. As a member of the same family Columcille was under an obligation to seek the proper compensation — the "blood-price" for the death of his kinsman. He was in a double-bind since as a church-man he was bound to defend the principle of sanctuary. If Diarmid's men attempted to drag Curnan from sanctuary it is more than likely that a struggle ensued which might have resulted in the death of one of the king's men.[2]

Whatever happened, it appears the situation escalated rapidly and ended in a battle fought on the lower slopes of Ben Bulben in Sligo resulting in the death of three thousand men[3] on Diarmid's side, and (according to Columba's biographer, one should note) only one on the side of the O'Neills. The battle is known as Culdreimhne (Coolrevne) and it was fought in 561 AD.

There is a story that Columba was advised by St Molaisse to undertake the conversion of as many souls as had been killed in the battle. (Several other saints have been credited with this advice, which suggests this story has gone a-wandering.)

However, there is a strong possibility that the two Columbas have somehow become confused and that the massacre of three thousand souls should be laid at the door of Columbanus rather than Columcille.

[2] Thomas Cahill offers a completely different version of events (*How the Irish Saved Civilisation*, p. 170) in which Columcille gets into trouble for copying a book without permission. The King in that case rules that he must give the copy back to the original book's owner — the first recorded copyright case. However it is difficult to see why this would lead to anyone's death as the king's judgement is perfectly fair. This story probably came into being rather later after the meeting at Drumceatt where Columcille defended the bards' right to freedom of speech as it seems connected to that. The story of the violation of the sanctuary given to his kinsman seems much more likely as this would certainly have escalated what appears to have already been a blood-feud and would almost inevitably lead to someone getting killed.

[3] One should be careful about numbers of casualties. In one account the figure is given as five thousand and due to inaccurate typing in an early draft of my notes I inflated it to 30,000. However the usual size of a shield army was around three thousand men so whatever the precise number of casualties the inference is that an entire army was wiped out in the engagement.

It is certainly true that Columba was at Culdreimhne and that his exile was somehow connected to something that took place there.

He wrote a poem describing his voyage into exile from which it is clear something pretty bad happened at Culdreimhne.

What is intriguing about this poem is that it contains no suggestion of a sense of guilt about what happened. Given that monks were inclined to self-recrimination this is surprising. Instead we are treated to a strong expression of a sense of injustice.

Columcille in Exile

It would be a pleasant thing
O Son of Man
To feel the waves beneath me swing
And swell as my ship before them ran
Back to Ireland.

To Eorlaig's plain, past Ben Evanagh
Across Loch Feval
And hear the swans in chorus there
Give their chorale.

And when my boat, the Derg Drulach
At last makes harbour, touches the shore
In Port na Ferg, to be welcomed back
By my own people of Foyle once more.

I am always longing for Ireland, the land
Where I had power.
An exile now, among strangers, unmanned
I cry every hour.

Woe to those that forced this journey upon me
O King of my heart.
Would to God I had never gone to Culdreimhne.
In tears I part
From the land I love, the land of Ireland.

To sleep at Comgall's, to visit Canice —
Those were good times. That was peace.[4]

What ever Columcille was accused of he clearly believed he was innocent. Whatever had happened he had been forced into it.

---

[4]   Author's version, but see also Brown, 2006, p. 106.

He certainly didn't go willingly into exile with a view to converting three thousand souls to Christianity. He leaves nursing a strong sense of grievance.

Initially the sentence that was passed on him by the synod of Teiltu was not exile but excommunication. This would have effectively ended his career in the Church. It's a fair guess that it was this synod that stripped him of the name Columcille — Colum of the Church — and insisted he was renamed simply Columba.

In the light of his subsequent activities, we may also wonder whether his exile was not also due to church politics. Since he was so able a churchman the severity of a sentence of excommunication perhaps explains why he argued strenuously to have it lifted. We are told it was lifted almost immediately and we can only suppose this was agreed because Columcille accepted instead the civil punishment for causing a death of ten years exile outlined above.[5]

Presumably he hoped even to escape this sentence because he doesn't seem to have left Ireland for another two years. When he left he didn't go alone but took with him twelve companions — the requisite number for founding a new monastery of which he clearly intended to be the head.

Nor did he go into permanent exile. Although technically he travelled out of sight of his native land, which was the minimum legal requirement, he didn't really leave Irish territory. He went to Dalriada — which is only just out of sight of Northern Ireland — indeed if you look at the map you will see that Iona is a relatively short distance from his beloved Lough Foyle and there must have been constant sea traffic between the two.

---

[5]   He was possibly able to argue that since it was a secular event the resulting crime came under the jurisdiction of a secular court and was thus a civil matter rather than an ecclesiastical one. The clergy usually argued the other way round as the ecclesiastical courts were inclined to be more lenient but in this case, for both personal and political reasons, the secular sentence was more acceptable to Columcille.

He sought help from his cousin, King Aedan mac Gabrain (Chadwick, 1970, p. 91),[6] who had established a kingdom of Scots having placated or overcome the native Picts. He granted Columcille land on Iona after his enemies in Ireland had complained that he had not gone far enough for his exile to be regarded as penitential. From Iona, Columcille insisted, Ireland was never in sight.

There he set up his famous monastery of which — again cocking a snook at the authorities who had tried to excommunicate him — he appointed himself the first Abbot.

That his punishment was for one death and not three thousand is evidenced by the fact that as soon as the ten years were up — one imagines him rushing to the harbour the very next day — he returned to Ireland to take part in a national conference at Drumceatt. He went ostensibly to argue on behalf of Dalriada that it deserved exemption from the payment of tribute to the High King of Tara. It was always a meaningful slap in the face for a Dark Age King to deprive him of taxation so Columcille must have enjoyed that.

On the ecclesiastical front we find him taking another swipe at the authorities by reverting to his original monastic name of Columcille and fighting the corner of the bards — whose propensity for satire we have already noted — who were in danger of suppression.

Our Columbanus was twenty years younger than Columcille but the two men had much in common. Columcille's mention of his friendship with Comgall in his poem on exile indicates that he was often at Bangor and it is inconceivable that Columbanus, a fellow poet and scholar, did not come into frequent contact with him. It is not unreasonable to suppose that he became embroiled in the same controversies and left Ireland under a similar cloud and for very similar reasons. There seems to have been a period of

[6]   Many authorities suggest the King in question was King Bruide but this seems to be a confusion of King Brude mac Maelchon, the King of the Northern Picts whose lands were to the north of Dalriada and Eochaid Buide, the son of Aedan mac Gabrain. He did not become King of Dalriada until after his father's death in 608 AD by which time Columcille had also died.

repression in Ireland at this time, with a concerted attack on freedom of speech, which both men would have found intolerable.

The Kings of Leinster and the Kings of Munster had been in constant conflict for centuries and, since we have already noted that Irish monks were still called up for military service, it's highly unlikely that Columbanus had reached his fortieth year without becoming embroiled in some battle or other.

As already suggested, it's possible that the story of the three thousand dead and the injunction to compensate for the deaths with the saving of a like number of heathen souls does not refer to Columba of Iona at all but to Columba the Younger, our Columbanus.

"Obey your superiors, lead your juniors and equal your equals", he wrote.[7] That sounds to me like a military man.

The large number of deaths involved (the exact number being immaterial) would explain why the sentence in the case of Columbanus was much more severe than that which we know Columcille actually served.

As another measure of how Irish law was implemented in such circumstances we can look to the case of two men, Snedgas and Mac Riagla, who were sentenced to death for the murder of King Domnall who reigned from 639 AD to 642 AD so only a generation after Columbanus' death.

Their sentence was commuted and instead they were set adrift to explore the outer sea and, we are told, found many wondrous isles (Johnson, 1997, p. 115).[8]

The decision to commute the sentence might be related to the later mediaeval practice of "benefit of clergy" whereby churchmen were entitled to be tried by ecclesiastical courts and regarded as outside the normal sphere of civil law. This generally meant a more lenient sentence although not if the charge was heresy (see p. 59, footnote 5).

---

[7] 'Letter to a young disciple' 610 AD, O'Fiach, 1990, p. 86.
[8] The original story comes from "The Voyage of Snedgrass and Mac Riagl" ("Immam Snedgusa ocus Maic Rigla"). This tale of pilgrimage may be fictional but there is no reason to suppose the background details are not accurate.

Snedgas and Mac Riagla were monks of Iona and in the case of Columcille, Columbanus and perhaps Brendan, the most famous navigator, the fact of their being monks might have influenced the nature of their punishment.

In the case of Columbanus, although not Columcille or Brendan, exile was permanent and, although at one point he was nearly repatriated, that was a forcible repatriation and his relief that he was not obliged to break his vow indicates that had he returned to Ireland he would not have been facing a hero's welcome. There is fairly good reason therefore for supposing his exile was no more voluntary than that of Columcille.

Of course it may be that his motives were, as Jonas suggests, much simpler. He was forty years old. His Abbot, Comgall, was in the rudest of health and there was no possibility of him becoming Abbot at Bangor for very many years to come. His best chance of promotion, to put it in worldly terms, was to take off and found his own monastery. In other words his motive was professional rather than personal. He was ambitious.

Or it may be that the forces that prompted his departure from Ireland were even more complex than either of the above. To see what these might have been we have to look more closely at the time-frame of his departure. When did Columbanus leave Ireland?

Chapter 6

When did Columbanus leave Ireland?

You promised me a thing that was hard for you,
A ship of gold under a silver mast,
Twelve towns with a market in each of them
And a fine white court by the side of the sea.[1]

The date usually given for the arrival of the Irish monks in France is circa 590 AD but this is also the date given for the founding of Luxeuil, which was Columbanus' second foundation, the first being at the old Roman hill-fort of Anagrates, modern Annegray.

Since the date for the founding of the third of the Irish foundations, Fontaine, is given as 592 AD and bearing in mind the two-year time-frame it took Columcille to set up his establishment on Iona, 590 AD looks like the probable date for the founding of Luxeuil particularly bearing in mind that when Columbanus writes to the Bishops of France in 603 AD he mentions that he has been there for 12 years (so he actually moved there in 591 AD).

Assuming that it took two years to set up Luxeuil work must have started on this foundation around 588 AD.

On this time-scale and working backwards work could not have begun on Anagrates much after 586 AD and Columbanus must have arrived in Europe some time before that.

---

[1] From "Donal Og", Anon., translated from the Irish by Lady Augusta Gregory.

There is good reason to suppose that work on Anagrates started slightly before 586 AD in the spring of the previous year in fact, early in 585 AD.

The Irish monks found conditions at Anagrates extremely difficult. Their project began well enough with them rebuilding the walls of the old fort and clearing and tilling the fields, which suggests they arrived in the sowing season, early in the year.

Then everything went wrong. Despite their best efforts they suffered a disastrous crop failure, so much so that they reported that they would have starved had it not been for the goodwill of the local Bishop who helped them out with cartloads of vegetables from time to time.

Jonas endows this timely assistance with the air of divine providence and indeed with hindsight it may have seemed that way. If we compare this with what Gregory of Tours tells us about conditions in Gaul in the year 585 AD it helps us to establish our time-line.

> In this year (585 AD) almost the whole of Gaul suffered from famine. Many people made bread out of grape-pips or hazel catkins, while others dried the roots of ferns, ground them to powder and added a little flour. Some cut green corn-stalks and treated them in the same way. Many others, who had no flour at all, gathered grasses and ate them, with the result that they swelled up and died. Vast numbers suffered from hunger to the point that they died. The merchants took sad advantage of the people, selling a bushel of corn or half a measure of wine for the third of a gold piece. The poor sold themselves into slavery in order to obtain something to eat (Thorpe, 1974, VII 45).

That the Irish arrived in Gaul at a time of famine suggests that they arrived at Anagrates, with high hopes of success, at the beginning of 585 AD.

The help they received from local people suggests they were not received with any serious hostility. Perhaps the fact that it was a time of famine was advantageous to them since the local population were moved by fellow-feeling to show them hospitality and help them out at this time of general suffering.

Their mutual discomfort and co-operation brought the two communities together in a time of trouble and the monks must have acquitted themselves well in the aftermath since they were made very welcome in the years immediately after.

So 585 AD would appear to be the year in which Columbanus and his companions struck out from the Austrasian (Eastern Frankish) court at Metz into the then fairly remote and well-forested hinterland of the Vosges mountains and began their mission in earnest.

But before that they had been at the Neustrian (Northwestern Frankish) court in Paris, prior to which they had landed in Brittany, so they must have arrived in Gaul (it was acquiring its modern name of Francia or France but Gregory, being of an old Roman senatorial family as he frequently reminds us, still refers to it by its Latin name of Gaul — hence things French or Frankish are also Gallic) in the middle of the previous year AD 584.

We can propose a date of late spring/early summer — say May/June for their arrival because in northern countries people rarely put to sea in the winter months. This date would also fit in with the theory that the sentence of permanent exile might have resulted from the part the monks had played in a major battle. Battles were fought in the time between sowing and harvest. The bulk of the troops were tenant farmers or farm workers and if called up at those times they were apt to melt away at the first opportunity and go back to their fields. This was a perennial problem for a feudal army.

It's a reasonable guess then that Columbanus and his party set out from Ireland sometime in early summer 584 AD.

Their route would have taken them at first across the Irish Sea to the Isle of Man, then to Holy Island off Anglesey. The Irish Sea although not wide is quite treacherous and, if they were sailing in a curragh, a light shallow-draught craft constructed of animal hides dried on a timber frame designed for fishing and coastal traffic, island-hopping would be the safest way to cross the ocean. They would have proceeded

Columbanus

Route Columbanus took to Brittany

to Bardsey Island where St Cadfan, originally choosing to live on the island as an anchorite, founded his monastery in 516 AD.

The four-mile stretch of sea between Bardsey and the mainland of Wales is one of the most dangerous in the world. From Bardsey they would have been able to take advantage of the shelter of Cardigan Bay making for St David's. We have already noted several times the importance of St David's in the life of Irish monks.

From St David's they appear to have followed a perfectly straight course across the mouth of the Bristol Channel to Newquay in North Cornwall landing in the centre of what is now Watergate Bay. The villages of St Columb Major and St Columb Minor traditionally mark the route they took which indicates they then took the land route across the peninsula to St Austell.

There would have been no shortage of Celtic brothers and sisters to offer them hospitality along the way because the peninsula is littered with villages named in their honour — St Enoder, St Dennis, St Stephen, St Blazey all mark the road to St Austell so our little band of travellers were not short of like-minded company.

From St Austell they would have found passage — perhaps on a slightly bigger ship, one of the Breton style galleys[2] that carried cargoes between Britain and its namesake Brittany and down to Bordeaux, by which means they crossed the Channel, again by a direct route, and landed at Dinard where Malo — still alive and kicking so not yet a saint — was Abbot.

---

[2] Although it is known that Columcille travelled the short distance to Dalriada in a curragh we should not assume that Columbanus made the longer journey to the continent by the same means. Even in 56 BC the Bretons were notable ship-builders. Their ships are described by Caeser as having thin leather sails designed to resist the Atlantic gales, the ships built of oak and "as high and massive as citadels", the benches made of planks a foot wide "fastened by iron nails as thick as a man's thumb". In the naval battle of Morbihan Bay they were defeated by the Roman galleys which were lighter and lower and more manoeuverable but it is likely that for longer sea-voyages on the Atlantic coast Breton ships of the more stable and robuster design were still in use in the sixth century.

The village of Cancale about six miles east of present-day St Malo (which did not of course bear that name while the saint was still alive) has a granite cross which traditionally marks the site where Columbanus and his party landed. Given its proximity to present-day St Malo this is a reasonable claim.

This journey, allowing for the speed of travel by water and overland, must have taken them several weeks but even so it's a fair assumption that they made landfall on the continent by midsummer of 584 AD.

As to what happened then accounts vary.

It is generally agreed they were invited to meet the King of Neustria at his court which according to Jonas was being held in Reims but which King?[3]

Some versions, taking the date of their arrival as circa 590 AD suggest they received an invitation from Lothar II, as he was strictly speaking the King of the Northern Franks at this date.

Slight snag. At this date Lothar II was only six years old and his interest in theological matters must have been rather limited. This being the case, other historians, having noticed the improbability of his issuing the invitation, suggest that it was extended rather by his uncle, King Guntram, who was technically King of Burgundy — then the southern Frankish kingdom with its capital at Arles — but who, because of his nephew's extreme youth, was at that date acting as his regent and *de facto* King of Neustria as well.

This seems more probable except that Guntram showed no more interest in theological disputes than his six year-old nephew. He adopted the same pragmatic attitude to religion as he did to everything else. He took the line of least resistance and kept his nose clean. Nor, prior to 585 AD,

---

[3]   As with all mediaeval monarchs the court of the Frankish kings was peripatetic. The principal "capitals" for Neustria were Soissons and Paris. The kings of the Eastern Frankish kingdom (Austrasia) favoured Reims and Metz (although note the way in which the kings shared cities between them — all three kings regarded Reims as an important capital). Jonas assumes the king was Sigibert (King of Austrasia) and therefore that the court was held at Reims but the monks would have to pass through Neustria to get there.

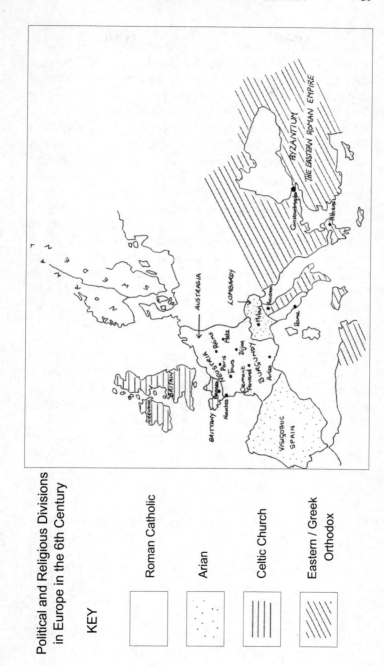

Political and Religious Divisions
in Europe in the 6th Century

KEY

Roman Catholic

Arian

Celtic Church

Eastern / Greek
Orthodox

does he appear to have spent much time at Reims. He was based either at Arles or Clermont Ferrand in the south. Indeed we know from Gregory that he specifically came north in the autumn of 585 AD so had not been there all summer (Thorpe, 1974, p. 391).

So neither of these kings looks a likely candidate.

The problem has arisen because previous commentators have stuck to the date of AD 590 as the date around which the Irishmen landed. Jonas of Susa says the king who invited the local party was Sigibert but he had been assassinated as early as 575 AD and that date does not fit our time-line for the foundation of Annegray at all.

If we wind back to AD 584 the picture becomes much clearer and altogether more interesting. Jonas was right. It was neither Lothar II nor Guntram who invited Columbanus to his court but one of the earlier Frankish kings. It is understandable that Jonas should assume it was Sigibert given the close relationship Columbanus developed later with his widow and son, but since it cannot have been him that leaves only one candidate.

The King who invited Columbanus to his court was Lothar's father, King Chilperic, and it was not Reims that he invited them to, although that was the city which all the Frankish kings regarded as their principal capital, because he was not there at the time. He was in Paris.

There is good reason for believing this is the case. Neither Lothar nor Guntram was directly embroiled in religious controversy at this date but Chilperic certainly was.

At this time Christianity in Europe was fairly evenly divided into three factions; Celtic Christianity — mostly in Great Britain, Ireland and Brittany; Roman Catholicism which survived as a legacy of the fading Western Empire and maintained the administrative structure and authoritarian hierarchy of the imperial model; and Unitarian Arianism, which had come from the East, like the Coptic Christianity that infused the British and Irish churches, with persecuted refugees.

The Visigothic kings had embraced this brand of Christianity as their official religion. So in Visigothic Spain and

Lombardy in Northern Italy Arianism was the dominant style of theology. In still culturally Roman Gaul the metropolitan bishops of the Roman Catholic Church were pre-eminent but by no means predominant. The metropolitan bishops, as the name suggests, were powerful men in the cities but in the countryside there were still many pagans — the Latin *pagani* means 'rustics' — both of the Graeco-Roman variety and the Franco-German invaders, not to mention pockets of druidism, the religion of the native inhabitants of ancient Gaul.

The philosophical distinctions between the three main Christian sects are extremely fine and we will struggle with them soon enough, but at this point let's just say there were three churches.

The Frankish kings had accepted the self-evident pre-eminence of the metropolitan bishops who all came from the old Roman senatorial families. Gregory mentions that nearly all the bishops in the See of Tours which included Le Mans, Angers and Poitiers, were his blood-relations. This means his family had a firm grip on the whole region and this pattern was repeated across Gaul.

Given that the administrative and economic structures of Gaul were still Roman, the Frankish Kings wisely accepted that their power depended on co-operation with and the manipulation of these old Roman political structures. Accordingly they nominally accepted Roman Catholicism and upheld it as the official religion of the state while still maintaining, in spite of their presence at Christian ceremonies, their old pagan habits of polygamy. Although some kings, like Sigibert, who married only one wife, and his son Childebert (who married several) were sincere in their espousal of Christianity, for others like Chilperic and Guntram it was largely a matter of political convenience and their allegiance to the Roman Catholic Church was based on expediency. This meant, as Gregory and the other metropolitans knew well, that their loyalty was fragile and inconstant.

The Franks held most of what is now modern France (except Brittany which remained an independent Celtic nation), modern Belgium and the Netherlands up into Northern Germany, a narrow corridor down both sides of the Rhine and a large part of modern Switzerland. They therefore controlled a very large part of that territory to which the papacy could reasonably lay claim.

In Italy itself the "Papal States" were confined to the south and west — the area around Rome itself. Ravenna and the eastern half of Italy including Sicily belonged to the Eastern Empire where Greek orthodoxy reigned supreme. The northern provinces including Genoa and Milan were part of Arian Lombardy. Roman Catholicism was not at that time by any means secure.

The roots of Chilperic's involvement in religious controversy went back a few years and had very little to do with his personal conscience. Nominally Roman Catholic, he had three wives and politically he was an amoral opportunist.

The famine of 585 AD was not the first and it's interesting to us to note that Europe at this period appears to have been going through a period of climate change. Gregory records many unusual meteorological events and there was a series of disastrous crop failures. This meant Chilperic was short of money and for a Dark Age King whose reputation and power rested on his role as the "gift-giver", the man who doles out treasure to his supporters, an empty treasury was a recipe for disaster.

In the previous year he had tried to solve his financial problems by levying a new series of taxes which made the tax burden so heavy it provoked a violent backlash. Gregory tells us:

> As a result a great number of people emigrated from their native cities or from whatever bits of land they occupied and sought refuge elsewhere, for they preferred to go into exile rather than endure such punitive taxation (Thorpe, 1974, p. 292).

In Limoges this ill-feeling erupted in street protests:

> A mob gathered; the people seized the tax-collector's demand-books and burned them to ashes. The king was furious. He sent his officials to Limoges and inflicted terrible punishments upon the populace (*ibid.*).

Not only did this make Chilperic politically unpopular it seemed to have terrible personal consequences also. An epidemic of dysentery broke out and took the life of his two younger sons.

Gregory suggested to his face that this was divine retribution for the heavy yoke he had laid on his people and his wife Fredegund, distraught with anxiety, begged him to burn the tax records in order that her sons might live.

Equally upset, Chilperic did as he was told and threw the tax records in the fire, thus abandoning his policy, but his sons died anyway. If there was anything guaranteed to destroy what vestige of dwindling religious faith he had, this must surely have been it.

He was left with one son from his first marriage but his deranged wife, distraught and driven by jealousy to take revenge for the loss of her own sons on her step-son, had him murdered.

Chilperic was also under pressure from his brother and nephew who both seem to have been eyeing up the possibility of adding his estates to their own especially as he was now without a male heir so either of them could inherit.

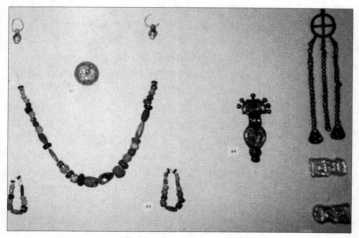

Frankish Ornaments of the 6th Century

Merovingian-Frankish fashion of this period copied the styles of the Eastern Empire.

Frankish politics are especially complicated by the fact that although the kingdoms can be roughly divided into east, west and south, in practice it wasn't like that at all. Each of the kings had territories within the other's kingdoms. Cities were carved up between them. So, for example, a row broke out (or was manufactured) between Guntram and Childebert about who owned which part of Marseilles. Marseilles, being in the south, was in Guntram's kingdom but Childebert owned a third of the city.

This odd pattern was repeated all over Gaul so it was an easy matter for one king to encroach on another's jurisdiction. There were constant squabbles between them as they took control of one another's cities. The fragility of his position encouraged Chilperic to look for an alliance with Visigothic Spain.

In the year 580 AD Leuvigild, the new King of Spain, had made overtures to Chilperic with a view of arranging a marriage alliance between his son Recared and Chilperic's daughter, Rigunth. The price of this marriage seems to have been a general conversion of the royal family and a transfer of the state religion from Roman Catholicism to Arianism.

Gregory reported ominously how the "Christians" of Spain were being persecuted (by Christians he means Catholics; it's a strange feature of Christianity that each of the different sects believes the others belong to a different religion entirely) and how the tax rises were being blamed on the "abbots and priests" who were accused of incitement (Thorpe, 1974, p. 301).

Leuvigild sends to Chilperic's court an Arian scholar Agilan whereupon the King manipulates Gregory into engaging into a dispute with him. Agilan claims that the Trinity represents three "Persons" inferring that the metropolitan Roman bishop is an old unreconstructed pagan who believes in many separate gods (*ibid.*, pp. 307–10).

Gregory stoutly defends his position by referring to the philosophy of St John. He accused Agilan:

> John the Evangelist says "In the beginning was the Word and the Word was with God and the Word was God. And the Word was made flesh and dwelt among us by whom all

things were made." You are so blinded by your poisonous heresy that you do not understand the Godhead (*ibid.*).

Agilan answered pointedly "Do you believe that the Holy Ghost is God, and do you maintain that He is equal to the Father and the Son?"

He points out that in the Gospels the Holy Ghost is "sent" by the Father and a person cannot send himself so God the Father and the Holy Ghost cannot be one and the same but must represent two separate entities. Surely Gregory must agree with this?

But the wily Bishop — slightly under five feet tall but not short of confidence — is not to be trapped so easily.

"In the Three there is one will, one power, one action", Gregory replies, "One God in Trinity and three Persons in Unity. There are three Persons but one kingdom, one majesty, one power, one omnipotence" (*ibid.*).

Agilan, Gregory tells us, lost his temper and the debate ended in acrimonious disagreement. He was annoyed presumably because he had failed to trip the bishop up. Whatever Gregory's failings, his theology was impeccable.

Agilan retreated with a plea for religious toleration. "You note", he reproved Gregory,

> that we who do not believe the things which you believe nevertheless do not blaspheme against them. It is no crime for one set of people to believe in one doctrine and another set of people to believe in another. Indeed, it is a proverbial saying with us that no harm is done when a man whose affairs take him past the altars of the Gentiles[4] and the Church of God pays respect to both.

But Gregory had heard about the persecution of the Catholics in Spain and he was not impressed by this burst of ecumenism.

It seems he was right to be wary, because Chilperic then issued a decree that there should be no distinction made between the three Persons in the Holy Trinity, but call it simply God, thus moving politically towards a rapprochement with the Arians.

----

[4]   By which he means the pagans.

Gregory maintained his stout defence. "What you say about the Persons", he lectured Chilperic, "must be interpreted spiritually not physically."

Chilperic had no answer to that. He blustered, "I will put these matters to men who are wiser than you."

If he hoped to put Bishop Gregory in his place he was out of luck because his first choice of referee, Bishop Salvius, was a fellow metropolitan and not surprisingly backed up his colleague.

For the moment Chilperic was stumped but he must have continued to nurture the hope of finding a scholar brilliant enough to defeat the wily Gregory.

That there may have been yet more behind this move to conciliate the Arian Visigoths is indicated in the following year when Chilperic's ambassadors returned from the Emperor Tiberius (Thorpe, 1974, p. 302).

We have a tendency in the West to lose interest in the Roman Empire after 475 AD when it ceased to dominate the political landscape of Western Europe but in 585 AD it was still very much alive and kicking in the East where the Greek-speaking Byzantines still called themselves Romans (rather perversely in Greek — *Romanoi*) although by practically everyone in western Europe they were referred to as "the Greeks".

The Roman Empire was by no means dead. The Eastern Empire was fabulously wealthy. It had largely given up seeking a military solution to the problem of its declining influence in the west apart from the occasional expedition to defend its territories in eastern Italy and Sicily. The Emperors were content to use their wealth to pull strings and influence affairs in the west to their own advantage.

We should not therefore be surprised that under considerable pressure Chilperic was making overtures to Tiberius seeking an imperial alliance. For a start the returning ambassadors eased his financial problems by bringing with them substantial gifts of gold as a gesture of goodwill.

That Gregory draws our attention at this point to the interference of the Eastern Empire in the affairs of the West opens up a whole new raft of possibilities and brings another complex web of political machinations into an already crowded frame.

In our story we have to remember that there are two Gregorys, Bishop Gregory of Tours and Pope Gregory I, also known as Gregory the Great.

In the year 580 AD the latter was neither Pope nor acknowledged as Great but he was in Constantinople, where the year before he had been sent to the Emperor Tiberius II by Pope Pelagius II as ambassador to the imperial court.

A link between Pope Pelagius II and our wandering Irish monks has never been explored because of that inconvenient arrival date of circa 590 AD. In that year Pope Pelagius II died of bubonic plague but in 580 AD he was still alive and in control.

His choice of papal title is intriguing because popes usually choose the name of someone they admire. Pelagius, to be sure, was an early Christian martyr, but it was also the name chosen by a British monk, presumably Welsh[5] since his family name was Morgan, who championed a Christian view that defended the freedom of the individual and the saving power of good works, thus restating the Celtic belief that there was a direct relationship between the individual and God and that the intercession of the church was not the only path to enlightenment.

This, not surprisingly, didn't go down well with the Church Fathers who condemned Pelagius as a heretic but the "Pelagian heresy" continued to dog Catholicism all down the Middle Ages.

Although the Roman Church condemned Pelagius for his ideas the Celtic Church was shot through with them.

It's noticeable that throughout this period the popes were divided between those who took a tolerant view of differing points of view in doctrinal matters, and with whom Columbanus seems to have been on quite friendly terms, and those like Boniface IV who sought unity by enforcing

[5]   Strictly speaking he was British as Wales as a nation did not yet exist but the name suggests he came from what is now Glamorgan

ideological conformity, and with whom Columbanus came intellectually to blows.

Respect for differences was written into the rule books of Irish monasteries and for Columbanus it was a rule that was unbreakable (Cahill, 1995, p. 176).

The row between Columbanus and Boniface IV (who was Pope 608–615 AD) centred on the Three Chapters Controversy referring to a section of the legal Code of the Emperor Justinian.

Although its theology is tortuous the political purpose of this section of the codex is very clear.

Its aim was to appease the Monophysites (who for our purposes are pretty much the equivalent of the Arians in the west) and by unifying belief and welding the Christian Church into a homogenous instrument of rule reunite the Eastern and Western Empires under a single Christian banner.

In other words what had been lost militarily could be regained through the spread of a unified ideology. For decades the Eastern and Western churches had been in schism over this "Three Chapters Controversy" but the dream of reunification continued to shape catholic policy right through the Middle Ages at least until the fall of Constantinople in 1453 AD.

In 580 AD barely more than a hundred years since the deposition of the last Western Emperor, the dream was even more alive since the Pope in Rome was not an independent authority but answerable still to the Emperor in Constantinople, one of five patriarchs, the other four being all in the East, from Alexandria, Antioch, Constantinople and Jerusalem respectively.

The power of the metropolitan bishops in Gaul, preserving as it did the political and administrative structure of the Roman Empire was an important factor in the game-plan of the Eastern Emperors. They could not afford to allow this to be destroyed since if it were the rebuilding of the Empire in the west would have to begin again from scratch. As long as the Emperors had a grasp on the Roman Catholic Church and could maintain its power and influence there was at least a chance that the old boundaries of Roman influence could once more be established in the west.

It is no wonder then that, given Chilperic's apparent move towards creating an alliance with Visigothic Spain which would embrace Arianism as the state religion, the Eastern Emperor was making a bid to buy back his favour.

As part of his bid to achieve religious uniformity Chilperic's next act was to try and enforce the conversion of the Jews. This was probably motivated more out of a desire to extract bribes out of them and find an excuse to confiscate their property since Chilperic was at the time again rather hard up. The erratic weather pattern and repeated crop failures meant that, although he had endeavoured to reform the system of taxation, the taxable income of his estates continued to fall.

He tried to prohibit the granting of legacies to the Church, a practice which created land grants that were inalienable and tax-free. Such grants not only depleted the amount of land available for royal taxation, it was at the same time the source of the enormous economic power of the Bishops. In this case the Bishops won the argument and fortunes continued to be willed to swell the wealth and power of the Church and be a bone of contention between the spiritual and temporal powers of Europe right down to the Reformation.

What is clear is that Chilperic was aiming at a degree of religious conformity which would subject the power of the Church to secular authority. In other words religion would be state-controlled. Again this battle between the sovereignty of the civil government and the over-arching authority of the church in both civil and religious matters continued to echo down the ages and was not resolved in France until the Revolution. When you consider that this did not occur even in rebellious Britain until the time of Henry VIII, it would be fair to say that Chilperic was a man well ahead of his time.

How far he was really serious in this intention and how much it was simply designed to annoy and undermine the metropolitan bishops is a moot point. Chilperic was not a man of faith. He had no great ideological axe to grind. His policies were a response to the economic difficulties and political realities of the moment.

However, in considering when and why Columbanus left Ireland and made his way to the court in Paris we have to allow for the possibility that he went because Pelagius II, a Pope sympathetic to the cause of the Celtic Church and seeing an opportunity to extend its influence, had asked him to.

On 1 September 584 AD an embassy came from Visigothic Spain to collect Chilperic's daughter Rigunth, who was about to be despatched to meet her future husband Recared the son of the Arian King Leuvigild with an enormous amount of treasure (Thorpe, 1974, p. 377).

Like many another bride's father before and since, Chilperic found himself nearly cleaned out. He was further startled when his wife Fredegund piled on another lot of treasure. Seeing her husband (and his nobles who might have expected a share in it) deeply upset she reassured everyone that this treasure was her own, although she did not specify how she had come by it . Bearing in mind she had started her married life as a servant in his household, the suspicion arises that she had not come by it exactly honestly.

Chilperic took the opportunity to relieve himself of some of his economic burden by forcing large numbers of the serfs from his estates, for whose support he was responsible, to emigrate along with his daughter. Gregory tells us that some who were quite well-born were also despatched, which must have been an opportunity to get rid of a few trouble-makers.

The scene was dreadful. "They say that quite a few of the serfs hanged themselves in their distress", says Gregory. "Sons were torn from fathers, mothers were separated from their daughters." With some satisfaction he points out that many of them left their property to be conveyed to the church in the event that they were unable to return from Spain, thus preventing Chilperic from getting his hands on it.

Into all this chaos strolled our wandering Irish monks, perhaps not wandering quite so aimlessly and artlessly as Jonas suggests.

If Columbanus was to have acted as referee in another staged theological dispute between the Romans and the Arians he never got the opportunity. While the wedding party plundered its way through Gregory's See, behaving more like an invading army than a bridal procession, Chilperic took a short break from his troubles and went hunting at his estate at Chelles between Paris and Senlis.

While he was there he was struck down by an unknown assassin.

What does this have to do with Columbanus? It's unlikely that he committed the murder as he is practically the only person in our story who doesn't have a motive. After all, he was hoping that Chilperic would be able to help him with a grant of land to set up his foundation. And yet ...

Jonas does tell us that the King begged him to remain at the court and promised that he and his monks could have whatever they wanted. It was a pretty good offer.

When Columbanus politely declined and reiterated his intention to take his mission into the wilderness the King then delivered a darker message.

> If you wish to take up the cross of Christ and follow him, look for a more secluded place of retreat, but do not leave our territory, nor pass to neighbouring peoples ... (Jonas, p. 6).

It appears that the Irishmen for some reason were being placed under a form of house arrest.

Dumping someone in a remote monastic establishment was a convenient form of imprisonment. But why should Chilperic have objected to them moving on? And whatever his reason, was this the occasion of a quarrel between two quarrelsome men? Perhaps it is a step too far to suggest that Columbanus was himself guilty of the king's assassination. Although we know he had a violent Irish temper (in South Wales for obvious reasons such a temper has always been known as a "Mick") the murder seems to have been premeditated and that wasn't his style.

But what happened subsequently suggests that if Columbanus did not commit the murder he had a very good idea who did.

So who did murder Chilperic?

Chapter 7

The Sons of Lothar

As the year 584 AD got under way it seemed as if things had been leading up to some momentous event. The changing climate had continued to create havoc horticulturally.

Roses, Gregory assures us, had flowered in January (although he doesn't say how far south). A great circle, he tells us "of many colours, like one sees in a rainbow after a heavy downpour" appeared around the sun. Frosts caused serious damage to the young vines which, if that were not bad enough, were then severely battered in a violent hailstorm. If any crops at all survived the tempest they were then destroyed by a fierce drought (Thorpe, 1974, p. 377).

Men he says "were so furious with God that they left the gates of their vineyards wide open and drove in their cattle and horses."

Trees which had borne apples in July had a second crop in September. One epidemic after another killed off the flocks until hardly any remained alive. Small wonder then that Chilperic decided to take some time off.

Gregory tells us then exactly what happened.

> One day when he returned from hunting just as twilight was falling, he was alighting from his horse with one hand on the shoulder of the servant, when a man stepped forward, struck him with a knife under the armpit and then stabbed him a second time in the stomach. Blood immediately streamed from his mouth and through the gaping wound and that was the end of this wicked man (*ibid.*, p. 379).

The groom appears to have been the only person with the King which suggests that whoever it was that approached him, Chilperic thought he had nothing to fear. He had already taken precautions against possible assassination

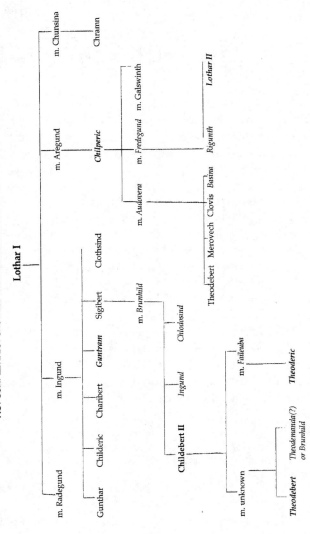

THE FAMILY TREE OF LOTHAR I

NOT COMPLETE BUT SHOWING THE SURVIVING FAMILY OF LOTHAR II IN ITALICS

attempts ordered by his brother Guntram so it's surprising to find him meeting someone without a bodyguard.

Had he arranged a secret meeting with Columbanus in order to bribe him to stitch up Bishop Gregory?

If so there may very well have been an altercation and since both men are known to have had violent tempers they may well have come to blows, but the groom did not apparently mention any argument, or even a conversation taking place. It all happened quickly and, apart from offering the vague information that the assailant was a man, the groom appears to have provided very little in the way of identification.

Was the finger of suspicion pointed at the Irish? After all they were strangers in the court and if the battle theory is correct they had arrived, having been expelled from their native land for an act of extraordinary violence, with a reputation for toughness.

There was also the matter of their appearance.

The Celtic monks favoured a different form of tonsure from the Romans. Instead of the pudding-bowl haircut and circular bald patch familiar to us from the later middle ages, they shaved the front of their heads from ear to ear and let their hair grow long at the back. It has been suggested that this made them look very odd but Chinese warrior-monks of the tenth century sported a very similar coiffure and, as witnessed by recent film constructions of the period, they looked perfectly fine.

More to the point, though, is the fact that it made them look — to someone who has only caught a brief glimpse of a hooded figure wielding a knife — quite similar to members of the Frankish royal family. The Frankish kings also wore their hair long tied with a sort of top-knot on the crown but this choice seems to have been not a whim of fashion but a mark of status and the style was exclusive to men of the royal family or their immediate kin.

Gregory tells us that when the Pretender Gundovald was repudiated by Lothar and then by Guntram on both occasions he was forced to have his long hair cut (*ibid.*, p. 349, S.19 & p. 374, S.41).

If the murder was committed by one of Chilperic's blood-relations then it might have been very convenient to suggest that the long-haired assassin came from among the group of wandering monks. It certainly seems that Columbanus and his companions didn't wait around for the charges to stick. We next hear of them in the jurisdiction of Childebert.

It was not too difficult for the assassin to get away. The hunting lodge at Chelles was a few miles outside the town of Senlis and Senlis was one of those towns with divided jurisdiction. One third of it belonged to Chilperic and two-thirds to Childebert. It was an easy matter to cross from one jurisdiction into another.

But there's no reason to get too hung up on the idea that the assassin was to be found among the long-haired strangers, because if we follow the usual practice of television detectives and start our investigation by asking "Who had a reason to want Chilperic dead?" the answer is "Practically everybody".

To find out how he had achieved this spectacular unpopularity we need, as screenwriters say, to fill in the back story.

The Kings of the Merovingian dynasty ruled over Gaul from the early fifth century down to 751 AD when the Carolingian dynasty took over. The earliest kings, like Arthur in Britain, are half-legendary but the first king to unite Gaul under the rule of the Salian Franks was Clovis.

Frank meant—and in English still does—free. In the prologue to their Salic law (which you will remember as banning Edward III from inheriting the throne of France through his mother and sparking the Hundred Years War) they described themselves as

> the glorious people, wise in counsel, noble in body, radiant in health, excelling in beauty, daring, quick, battle-hardened … this is the people that shook the Romans from its neck (Durant, 1950, p. 88).

The Romans might have regarded them as barbarians but there doesn't seem to have been much wrong with their self-image.

Clovis, as was the custom, divided his kingdom between his several sons which led to the equally customary round of sibling rivalry and civil wars until, by dint of being the last man standing, the country was again reunited under his youngest son Lothar I.[1]

Lothar in turn upon his death divided the kingdom between his sons of whom he had seven by different wives. Three predeceased him and Charibert died early on so we are mainly concerned with the two remaining sons from his first wife, Sigibert and Guntram, and a younger brother, the only child of his second wife, Chilperic.

There was also a pretender, Gundovald, whom I have already mentioned, who claimed to be Lothar's son by an unnamed woman. Lothar denied paternity and refused to acknowledge him, as did Guntram and he went off to live in the Eastern Empire but that was not the last they heard of him so we can't leave him out of our story.

Upon Lothar's death Chilperic made a dash to grab the treasury and put himself ahead of the field but his brothers weren't having any of that; after no doubt an interesting family row it was agreed to divide the kingdom fairly between them.

On the death of Charibert it was again partitioned, this time between the three remaining brothers. Chilperic inherited the kingdom of Neustria — the North-west kingdom with its capitals at Soissons and Paris, Sigibert inherited the Eastern Kingdom — Austrasia — with its capitals at Metz and Reims, and Guntram occupied the throne of Burgundy with his capitals at Arles in Provence and Clermont Ferrand in Puy-de-Dome.

However, as I have already pointed out, their property rights were not confined within the boundaries of their separate kingdoms and each of the brothers had jurisdiction all over the place.

Nor were they content to leave things as they were.

---

[1] The name is also spelt as Chlothar (and sometimes Clothaire) in older histories but I have followed the more modern usage. However for the sake of clarity Clothar, Clothaire and Lothar are all the same person.

While Sigibert was fighting the Hun on his eastern border Chilperic took the opportunity to attack Reims and a number of his other cities. Civil war broke out between the brothers and in retaliation Sigibert occupied Chilperic's capital of Soissons. There he found Theodebert, Chilperic's eldest son, and took him prisoner. He defeated Chilperic's forces and as a guarantee of his good behaviour kept Theodebert as a hostage for twelve months.

Sigibert was, Gregory tells us "a clement man" (unlike his brother) and so at the end of the year he sent Theodebert back to his father, thus endeavouring to set a good example in family relations (Thorpe, 1974, pp. 218–23).

Being a good Christian — indeed a good Catholic because Gregory totally approves of him — he also declined to follow his family's usual custom of polygamy.

King Sigibert, Gregory tells us, "observed that his brothers were taking wives who were completely unworthy of them and were so far degrading themselves as to marry their own servants." This last is a dig at Chilperic's second wife Fredegund who is described as having been a maid before her marriage.

Sigibert sent messengers loaded with gifts to Athanagild, King of Visigothic Spain, asking for his daughter Brunhild to be his wife. Although this was clearly a diplomatic arrangement — Athanagild sent his daughter with a large dowry — it seems also to have been a love match. Brunhild was elegant and beautiful and had brains as well as beauty. They married according to Gregory "with every appearance of joy and happiness" (*ibid.*, p. 221).

It was then Guntram's turn to try it on with his older brother. He occupied Avignon, which was Sigibert's city although close to his own capital, whereupon Sigibert retaliated by occupying Arles.

After the usual alarms and excursions each brother agreed to give back the other's city and the status quo was restored.

Chilperic then occupied Tours and Poitiers which were Sigibert's towns provoking another civil war. This time Guntram was inclined to side with Chilperic but Sigibert was having none of that. "If you do not permit me to pass through the lands which you have inherited so that I may cross this river", he said, when Guntram refused to allow his forces to cross the Seine, "I will turn my whole force on you" (*ibid.*, p. 246).

Guntram thought better of it. The dominant character of his older brother prevailed. His alliance with Chilperic crumbled and Chilperic, finding himself with now two brothers against him "took refuge with his wife and sons inside the walls of Tournai."

Sigibert then set about besieging his brother to force him into submission. St Germanus, the Bishop of Paris, made a dire prediction of the outcome of all this fraternal wrangling.

"If you set out", he said sternly,

> with the intention of sparing your brother's life, you will return alive and victorious. If you have any other plans in mind you will die. That is what God announced through the mouth of Solomon. 'Whoso diggeth a pit (for his brother) shall fall therein'(*ibid.*, p. 247).

Sigibert alas took no notice. He assembled his entire army around him at the royal Villa at Vitry where Gregory tells us "they raised him on a shield and elected him their king."

This moment of hubris was to be his undoing. Two young men who, according to Gregory, had been suborned by Queen Fredegund, came up to Sigibert carrying the strong knives which were commonly known as scramaxes and which they had smeared with poison.

They pretended they had something to discuss with the king and then struck him from both sides. He gave a loud cry and fell to the ground. He died soon afterwards.

And so began the long feud between Brunhild and Fredegund, between the royal house of Austrasia and the royal house of Neustria.

Our wandering monks had been invited to the court of Neustria but next we find them under the patronage of the court of Austrasia. To be sure the murder must have plunged the court at Paris into a state of turmoil but if they had gone there hoping for a grant of land on which to set up their first foundation why didn't they stay?

And perhaps more to the point, in spite of several attempts to encourage him with offers of money and land, why did Columbanus never go back?

Chapter 8

The Nero and Herod of Our Times

Before we examine our list of suspects we need to look a little more closely at Chilperic's impressive career.

You musn't run away with the idea that a couple of civil wars and the odd assassination were in themselves enough to earn him the epithet, or rather epitaph, that Gregory of Tours pronounced upon him — "the Nero and Herod of our Times" (Thorpe, 1974, p. 379).

He was "Nero" because, perhaps rather surprisingly, he was a keen amateur poet. Gregory tells us that he wrote two books, taking Sedulius as his model. Sedulius was a sixth century Christian poet who wrote in Latin but was perhaps Irish as there is a school of thought which suggests his name is a Latin version of the name Siadal (*ibid.*, p. 312).

This is interesting on two counts because, although according to Gregory, for whom Latin was his mother tongue, Chilperic's verses were "feeble and had no feet to stand on: he put short syllables for long ones, and long syllables for short ones not knowing what he was doing" (*ibid.*, p. 380), the King was writing in his second language and, if Sedulius was indeed Irish, presumably so also was he. Perhaps he was the chosen model for this reason.

Columbanus too was a notable poet writing in Latin, a language not his mother tongue, and Chilperic's poetic ambitions are noteworthy as this provides us with another reason to suspect he was the king who invited the Irish scholar-poet to visit him. They had a common love of literature. Chilperic also, Gregory tells us, composed some other short pieces, hymns and sequences for the Mass, and Columbanus we know did the same.

Sadly none of Chilperic's works have survived. They may indeed have been execrable as Gregory suggests but it would have been interesting to see them. He also apparently wrote verses in his native Frankish which must have been some of the earliest vernacular poetry to have been written down in that language; so however bad it may have been, it would have been a valuable source of literary history if it had been preserved.

Very few documents have survived from that period, probably because following the Roman custom they were still written on papyrus scrolls and papyrus does not last well in a damp northern climate (*ibid.*, p. 259).[1] Most surviving mediaeval documents were written on vellum (which is calfskin) or parchment (which is sheepskin) and better able to withstand the depredations of a damp atmosphere. Even so, most of those we have date only back as far as the ninth and tenth centuries. The earliest books of this type, the *Book of Durrow* and the *Lindisfarne Gospels*, were created in the seventh century. So when judging the literary and documentary output of the fifth and sixth centuries we have to bear this in mind. It was not an illiterate society. It is simply that the documents have not survived the passage of time.

Chilperic's hostility to the church had one unfortunate consequence in that his literary output was never copied by the monastic scribes who have preserved what early works we have. Possibly Gregory's dismissive observations discouraged them from taking an interest.

Still it was an unusual enough hobby for a Frankish king for the critical bishop to mention the fact. Chilperic was not a barbarian but a cultured, educated man however badly behaved.

---

[1]   See Gregory's riposte to the Bishop of Nantes with whom he had fallen out: "Instead of bringing you cargoes of oil and other wares, its ships could have carried only papyrus which would have given you more opportunity for writing libellous letters to honest folk like me. As it is only lack of paper cuts short your long-windedness."

He also had a love of beautiful objects. Gregory also tells us how on a visit to the King's manor at Nogent-sur-Marne his host had showed him a great salver which he had made of gold encrusted with gems and which weighed fifty pounds.

However, the King to his credit had a broader purpose in commissioning the work than mere acquisitiveness. "I have had this designed," he told Gregory, "for the greater glory and renown of the Frankish people" (*ibid.*, p. 328).

Treasure for a Dark Age King was not only of ornamental value. It was the basis of power, and also, as with any government, a source of export income and employment. Chilperic admired the workmanship of the craftsmen of the Eastern Empire but he also recognised that his own Celtic and Frankish silver and goldsmiths were equally talented and it was for this reason that he encouraged them to copy the beautiful gifts that came from Constantinople. In this he was being a far-sighted and capable governor.

More ominously for Gregory the King was often heard to say:

> My treasury is always empty. All our wealth has fallen into the hands of the Church. There is no-one with any power left except the bishops. Nobody respects me as King, all respect has passed to the bishops in their cities (*ibid.*, pp. 247–9).

For this reason we need to be cautious in accepting Gregory's judgement at face value. Chilperic may have been an amoral chancer but he was no fool.

By 584 AD, in fairly desperate financial straits the King had started to take drastic steps to reverse that position. This time it was the Church that was under attack.

Then there were other personal issues to be resolved.

We know that when their backs were against the wall Chilperic and Fredegund favoured attack as the best form of defence because it was while they were besieged at Tournai that Sigibert had been assassinated.

How had they come to be besieged? We have already seen that Guntram, who had initially sided with Chilperic in what appeared to be a turf war, had changed sides. Why had he done so?

It's very clear that Chilperic was intensely jealous of Sigibert. According to Gregory he was near perfect and that would be enough to get up any brother's nose. Older than Chilperic, he seemed to have it all. Above all he had made a perfect fairy-tale marriage to the beautiful and intelligent Brunhild who had brought with her a substantial dowry and a useful political alliance.

Chilperic had done nothing of the kind. His first wife Audovera had borne him three sons and a daughter so by the 570s she must have been getting rather old for his tastes. He despatched her to a convent at Rouen where she remained for the rest of her life.

He then married a servant[2] girl named Fredegund but on seeing Brunhild he became jealous of Sigibert's good fortune and decided that he too would marry a princess.

Luckily Brunhild had an older sister named Galswinth who was unmarried and so Chilperic arranged with her father Athanagild, King of Spain, for a double marriage — the two sisters to the two sons of Lothar.

This seemed an admirable arrangement and Athanagild readily agreed sending his daughter with another large dowry to be Chilperic's wife (*ibid.*, p. 222).

It seems likely that since Galswinth was to convert from Arianism to Roman Catholicism as her sister had done that part of the deal was that Chilperic should put aside his other two wives. Audovera seems to have gone happily enough but Fredegund was clearly livid and had no intention whatsoever of giving up her status without a fight.

At first Chilperic seems to have been quite happy with Galswinth. Perhaps she was not quite as beautiful as her sister, since Gregory is not as complimentary about her, but she had rank and money and two out of three was not bad.

---

[2]   Perhaps we should be cautious in accepting Gregory's assertion that Fredegund was a "servant" — "lady-in-waiting" might perhaps be a better description, although the Frankish kings do not seem to have been at all snobbish in regard to their marriages

Unfortunately, not only does she seem to have lacked Brunhild's looks, she also lacked her character. Galswinth did nothing but complain, notably and specifically about the insults she had to put up with, presumably from Fredegund. Galswinth was converted to Roman Catholicism and anointed with the chrism. Having kept to her side of the bargain she had every reason to insist that Chilperic kept to his.

No-one can say what goes on in another person's marriage but we can guess that it went badly because Chilperic was soon back in the arms of Fredegund and his unhappy third wife announced her intention of returning to her father in Spain, although she prudently offered to leave her dowry where it was.

It seems a fair offer and it's difficult to see why Chilperic didn't just accept it. Perhaps he intended to, but Fredegund saw that even if Athanagild swallowed the insult to his daughter he would not allow them to keep the dowry; and if Chilperic lost the treasure, his followers would pretty soon know who to blame.

Fredegund resolved the problem in a practical way. She had Galswinth strangled in her bed.[3] Chilperic wept crocodile tears and, whether he knew she was behind the murder or not, within days was back with Fredegund.

Brunhild was naturally beside herself when she heard of the death of her sister and since she was now their kinswoman, Sigibert and Guntram were honour bound to avenge Galswinth's death. It was for this reason that Sigibert set about driving Chilperic out of his kingdom and why, when Guntram learned of his suspicions, he switched sides and turned against his younger brother.

When Fredegund, besieged in Tournai, organised the assassination of Sigibert she was making a last throw of the dice. She knew that if they were captured her life would not be worth a candle even if Chilperic managed to wriggle out of it.

---

[3] Gregory gives the honours to Chilperic but given the outcome and her subsequent career I would say Fredegund had the greater motive.

So Galswinth's murder went unpunished and it seemed as late as 584 AD that they had got away with Sigibert's assassination as well. Nonetheless Chilperic had stored up plenty of trouble for himself.

By Audovera he had three sons, Theodebert, Merovech and Clovis. We can judge his dynastic ambitions by the names he gave his sons. Merovech and Clovis were two of the legendary founders of the Frankish monarchy. Theodebert, who seems to have been his father's favourite, had been killed in the war against Sigibert. At that time Clovis was still in his teens but Merovech was a young man.

As soon as Chilperic and Fredegund heard of Sigibert's death they rushed out to retrieve the body and bury it hastily in the village of Lambres, hoping thereby to remove any evidence that might prove their involvement.

Chilperic then immediately seized Brunhild and banished her to the city of Rouen, probably to the same convent in which he had immured Audovera, and took possession of the treasure she had brought to Paris.

This proved to be a mistake because his son Merovech saw his opportunity to be a hero. Under the pretext of visiting his mother he went to Rouen where he joined Queen Brunhild and made her his wife (*ibid.*, pp. 255–6 & 267–82). Since her son by Sigibert, Childebert, was barely five years old, this marriage effectively made him King of Austrasia.

His father was bitterly angry (and perhaps secretly rather proud since it was exactly what he would have done). On the entirely hypocritical grounds that the marriage was against canonical law[4] (technically Brunhild and Merovech were related as she was his aunt by marriage) Chilperic

---

[4]   Gregory states that the marriage was "in defiance of custom and canonical law". By custom he means Frankish law. Frankish law and Roman law differed in the way they calculated consanguinuity; Frankish law incorporated a wider range of relations who were ruled out in marriage contracts. First cousins for example could not marry, whereas under Roman law they could, and close in-laws were counted as blood relations. Therefore although Brunhild was only related to Merovech by marriage and not strictly a blood relation she was regarded as a blood relation for the purpose of a marriage contract and therefore the match was too close.

marched with an army to Rouen to confront the happy couple.

They took refuge in the church of St Martin which Gregory helpfully tells us was built of wooden planks high on the city walls. Here they claimed sanctuary.

Chilperic did all he could to persuade them to come down and eventually, upon his solemn oath that he would not try and separate them, they did come down and he received them affectionately. They dined together and when he set off to return to Soissons he took Merovech with him.

His climb-down was not mere paternal affection. Despite her precarious refuge Brunhild had not been idle. In his absence her troops had assembled in Champagne and marched on Soissons driving out Queen Fredegund and Prince Clovis. Chilperic hastened to recover the city but the incident made him suspicious of Merovech so he had him placed under house arrest while he decided what to do next. In the end he did the usual thing and packed him off to a monastery in Le Mans, which was part of Gregory's See of Tours, so the chronicler was particularly well-informed about this whole episode.

Duke Guntram Boso, who was Sigibert's military commander, advised Merovech to seek sanctuary in the cathedral of St Martin of Tours. Gregory insists he gave in only under duress, but since he generally sides with Sigibert and his family we can take that with a pinch of salt. It must have delighted him to see Chilperic challenged by his own son.

Chilperic ordered Gregory to give him up, but the feisty little man stood firm on the principle of sanctuary. However, to avoid Tours being devastated by Chilperic's troops, Merovech resolved to return to Brunhild, encouraged by the rather inaccurate prediction made by a woman prophetess who lived near Tours that in that year Chilperic would die and he, Merovech would be king (*ibid.*, p. 270).

Merovech left the sanctuary but was captured by Herpo, one of King Guntram's captains. Merovech escaped from his custody and was able to return to Brunhild but his ambition to be King of Austrasia was severely dented because the Eastern Frankish nobles refused to acknowledge him as their King.

Bluff, forthright Guntram had outmanoeuvred him with the political sleight of hand that was his hallmark. He had lost both his own sons to dysentery and so announced that he would now make the fatherless Childebert his heir. "Let one single shield," he declared grandly, "protect us both and a single spear defend us" (*ibid.*, p. 275).

This must have been a blow to Brunhild's ambitions too, because she had probably seduced the impressionable Merovech into marrying her with a view to governing Austrasia herself through him. The Eastern Franks clearly would not accept a foreign woman in authority even as Queen Regent. While Childebert was a minor she needed another man to act as his guardian.

Guntram had seen through her tactics and cleverly installed himself as guardian and regent of his newly adopted son. This meant that he, not Brunhild and Merovech, now controlled Austrasia as well as Burgundy.

Guntram and Childebert sent messages to Chilperic demanding that he restore the territory which he had taken from "their" realm or "choose a spot for battle". Chilperic, Gregory tells us, took no notice as "he was busy building amphitheatres in Soissons and Paris for he was keen to offer spectacles to the citizens" (*ibid.*). This is another example of the ambivalence felt by the non-Roman citizens of north-west Europe towards their imperial predecessors. Chilperic greatly admired Roman culture.

Besides he had other problems. Praetextatus, the Bishop of Rouen, who had conducted the marriage of Brunhild and Merovech, was said to be bribing people against his interests. The bishop was found to have treasure in his possession entrusted to him by Queen Brunhild, the implication being that he was bribing people on her behalf (*ibid.*).

Chilperic dared not act too precipitously against a metropolitan who had the right to be heard in an ecclesiastical court, but he promptly confiscated the property and banished Praetextatus until his case could be heard by a council of bishops.

This inevitably led to another stand-off between Gregory and Chilperic. Gregory stoutly defended his fellow bishop, evading in the process an attempt by Fredegund first to poison him and then to bribe him. It did no good. Praetextatus was thrown into prison and then banished. On the plus side they both survived.

Merovech was then ambushed and, to avoid being delivered into the hands of his father and step-mother, he reportedly asked his servant to kill him being unable to fall on his own sword Roman-style.

Gregory darkly hints that this version of events was inaccurate and that he was in fact murdered on the orders of Queen Fredegund (*ibid.*, p. 282).

Two down, one to go.

Fredegund meanwhile was having problems of her own in securing her future. Her son Samson, who was born during the siege of Tournai, died before completing his fifth year and she herself was very ill.

She had two more sons, but I have already related how they died of dysentery despite her attempts to placate a vengeful god by burning the tax returns. This trio of losses seems to have unhinged her. She sent her step-son Clovis, now grown to manhood, to the area where the dysentery outbreak was most virulent in the hope that he would catch the disease and die of it (*ibid.*, p. 303).

He remained in the rudest of health.

Chilperic now recognised that Clovis was his only surviving son and heir so he invited him to Chelles. His abrupt elevation seems to have gone to his head. He blamed Fredegund for his brother's death and couldn't resist rubbing salt into the wound.

"I warn you", he told her, "you can expect no better fate yourself now that you have lost the hope through which you were to have reigned."

This was an accurate statement of the position but hardly diplomatic and Fredegund, still in a fragile nervous state after her double bereavement, worked herself into a fury.

She made a bad enemy. Clovis was accused of using witchcraft against her; his girlfriend and mother were tortured to make them confess to their part in this alleged conspiracy of the dark arts; Clovis was arrested and kept under close surveillance. Whether Chilperic ordered this for his own or his son's protection is not clear but either way it failed because Clovis died in custody stabbed to death.

His mother Audovera was reportedly murdered — although we have no information as to when or how — and his sister Basina was "tricked by the servants of Fredegund into entering a nunnery" (*ibid.*, p. 304).

This left Chilperic without an heir. He was forced to follow the example of Guntram and form an alliance with his nephew Childebert and declare him his heir.

"My sins have grown so great", he said, sorrowfully if accurately,

> that my sons have been taken away from me. I have no heir left except King Childebert, the son of my brother Sigibert. I confirm that Childebert shall inherit everything that I manage to keep under my control. All I ask is that for the term of my natural life I may be left to enjoy these things in peace and quiet (*ibid.*, p. 349).

Like he meant it. Childebert was now eleven years old and a year off his majority. In Frankish society boys came of age when they reached their twelfth birthday. Competition between the brothers for complete control became acute.

Chilperic summoned his general Duke Desideratus and ordered him to launch a savage attack on King Guntram informing Childebert that it was Guntram who contrived his father's murder. It was at about this time that he began to take precautions against an assassination attempt (*ibid.*, pp. 351 & 364).

Then everything changed again because in 582 AD the persistent Fredegund produced another son whom they named Theoderic. This led to an unusual outbreak of peace as Childebert was no longer Chilperic's heir.

A great ball of fire was observed in 583 AD on the 31st January. Chilperic must have hoped this presaged great things for his little son. But again fate in the form of dysentery intervened and the child died in 584 AD.

Again Fredegund became pregnant and gave birth to a son, named Lothar after his grandfather. This time the anxious parents were taking no chances (*ibid.*, p. 375). They told no-one of the birth and had the baby cared for at a country manor far away from the unhealthy streets of the cities.[5]

At the same time Chilperic was offending the clergy, persecuting the Jews, trampling on the rights of the Roman senatorial families, taxing them to the hilt and forcing his own tenants to emigrate.

So when we ask who had a motive to murder King Chilperic, it might be easier to ask "Who didn't?"

---

[5] They seem to have been so convinced that the secret had been kept that after Chilperic's death Fredegund startled Guntram by telling him that she was pregnant again. He was surprised because he knew that she had given birth just a few months earlier — Lothar was four months old at the time of his father's death — but it seems that Fredegund did not know that he knew and was preparing the ground for announcing to everyone that she had another son "through whom she hoped to reign".

Chapter 9

Who Murdered King Chilperic?

If Columbanus and his party were at Chelles or on their way there to meet Chilperic in the autumn of 584 AD it's not surprising that they found themselves, in spite of dark warnings of dire consequences if they left Neustrian jurisdiction, swiftly established at the court of Childebert II because he was on his way to meet them.

The young king had been conveniently at Meaux, a half-day's ride from Senlis, when he heard the news of his uncle's assassination.

He moved swiftly arriving at Chelles just too late to capture Queen Fredegund, who must have got wind of his coming, but in time to grab most of the royal treasury (Thorpe, 1974, pp. 390–1).

The Queen had taken as much as she could carry and legged it to Paris. As soon as she got there she sent urgent messages to Guntram begging him to come and protect her.

At Chelles Childebert found only the Bishop of Senlis, Mallulf, who had been kicking his heels at the gate for three days waiting for an audience with the King. He had been summoned to the manor, probably to administer the last rites and had arranged for the body to be laid out and appropriately dressed. When Childebert arrived he was conducting the requiem masses.

The body of the king was then laid in a boat and carried by water to Paris for burial in the Church of St Vincent (*ibid.*, p. 381).

It was probably because he was escorting the hearse and thus moving slowly that Childebert arrived at the gates of the city to find them barred against him and his uncle Guntram already firmly in control.

Guntram, we are told, mourned for his brother but he must have kept it short because he answered Fredegund's call for help pretty promptly. Childebert, at 15, was now a king in his own right, but he was still the adopted son of Guntram who had rights of paternity over him. Guntram now also adopted the four-month old Lothar. As the sole surviving adult in the family he was finally in a position, or so he must have believed, to control the whole of Francia.

"Men and women, all people present", he addressed the congregation in the cathedral in Paris rather grandly,

> I ask you to remain loyal to me, instead of assassinating me, as only recently you assassinated my brothers. Give me three years at least in which to bring up these two nephews of mine, who are my adopted sons, for otherwise it might well happen—and this I beg everlasting God not to permit—that I should be killed while they were still small children, and then you too would perish, for there would be no full-grown man of my line to protect you (*ibid.*, p. 393).

Possibly Gregory invented this speech but it has something of the character of Guntram about it, his disingenuousness for example—Childebert was no longer a small child—and his astute political acumen. It's possible, but unlikely, that Chilperic was murdered as a prelude to a popular political uprising, given the strength of disgruntlement expressed by nearly all his subjects. It's much more likely that Guntram's artless remarks were addressed not to the people at large so much as the senior clergy, who would have been present in the cathedral when he made his speech. Because, although Guntram must himself be a prime suspect, given the outcome and the fact that we know Chilperic had already taken precautions to protect himself against an assassination attempt by his brother, there were at least two other entirely separate conspiracies to consider.

Childebert at any rate had no doubt who was responsible.

"Hand over the murderess," he demanded of his uncle — meaning Queen Fredegund — "the woman who garrotted my aunt, the woman who killed first my father and then my uncle and who put my two cousins to the sword" (*ibid.*, p. 392).

Like Guntram he was being somewhat economical with the truth because, as we have seen, Merovech was killed at his own instigation; but he was making it clear that he was taking the loss of his uncle very personally indeed. He was making it a matter of a blood feud.

The behaviour of Fredegund, it has to be said, did nothing to allay anyone's suspicions. Gregory hints at her close relationship with the tax-collector Audo, suggesting obliquely that this was the source of the unexpected wealth she displayed in providing wedding gifts for her daughter (*ibid.*, p. 399). Other people must have thought the same because Audo came in for some very rough treatment and only escaped with his life by seeking sanctuary in the cathedral with the Queen.

Then there was the behaviour of her daughter Rigunth. While all this had been going on her wedding party had been rumbling along coming ever closer to the Spanish border but when she realised they were about to enter Spanish territory she began to prevaricate and delay her journey (*ibid.*, p. 393).

Did she have some foreknowledge of her father's impending assassination? Was she dawdling on the French side of the border just waiting for news so that once she heard he was dead she could turn around and return again to Paris with all the treasure? If so, it suggests a degree of premeditation on the part of Fredegund. She certainly knew the value of capturing the king's wealth. Gregory tells us that her first act was to invite the treasurer Eberulf to live with her. When he declined she accused him of murdering her husband (*ibid.*, p. 402).

Fredegund appears to have guilt written all over her and yet, when Guntram hustled her aside and sent her to live at the country manor of Reuil near Rouen, she took her own revenge for her husband's death by arranging the assassination of the Bishop of Rouen Praetextatus.

Immediately following Chilperic's death Praetextatus, whom you will recall he sent into exile for performing the marriage ceremony for Merovech and Brunhild, was allowed by Guntram to return to his See, pending a hearing before the Bishops' Council. Guntram accepted the principle that ecclesiastics should be tried before an ecclesiastical court.

At around this time Guntram fell seriously ill and, given that he was living in such fear of assassination that he never went anywhere without a bodyguard, poison must be suspected. Fortunately for him he recovered, but Praetextatus was not so lucky. Gregory gives us a very graphic account of his assassination.

> The day of our Lord's resurrection came round. Early in the morning Bishop Praetextatus hurried off to church to perform the holy offices. He began to intone the antiphones in their proper order according to custom. During the chanting he reclined on a bench. As Praetextatus rested on this bench there appeared a cruel assassin who drew a dagger from his belt and struck the bishop under the armpit. He cried out to the clergy who were present for help but of all those standing near not one came to his assistance. As he prayed and gave thanks to God the hands which he stretched out over the altar dripped with blood (*ibid.*, p. 463).

Gregory, at least, is in no doubt who gave the order for the assassination and loses no time in pointing the finger. Praetextatus, he tells us, was carried to his cell and laid in his bed. He hardly had time to make himself comfortable before he received an unwelcome visitor.

> Fredegund lost no time in coming round to see him. She was accompanied by Dukes Beppolen and Ansovald.
> "Holy Bishop," she said, "your flock and I should never have lived to see the day when such a crime as this should be committed and while you were performing the office too. I can only hope that the man who has dared to do such a thing will be discovered, and that he will be properly punished for his evil action."
> The Bishop knew that she was lying.

"Who else has done this thing", he answered, "but the person who has killed our kings, caused innocent blood to be shed not once but many times, and been responsible for so much evil behaviour in this realm?"

"I have experienced doctors in my household who can cure the wound", said Fredegund. "Do let them come and take care of you."

"God has decreed that I must be recalled from this world", answered Praetextatus. "As for you, who are the prime mover in these crimes, as long as you live you will be accursed for God will avenge my blood upon your head."

As soon as the Queen had left him, the Bishop put his affairs in order and then gave up the ghost.[1]

Those who doubt the efficacy of curses will be interested to note that the Queen died of moderate old age and in her own bed.

However she had not finished there. You can sort of see why she and Chilperic were a good match.

Romachar, the Bishop of Coutances, was sent to Rouen to arrange for Praetextatus' funeral. It was presumably he who informed Gregory that

... all the inhabitants of Rouen were greatly grieved and especially the Frankish leaders in the town. One of these leaders went to Fredegund and said: "You have been the cause of much evil in this world, but you have never done anything worse than this, when you ordered one of the Lord's bishops to be murdered. May God be quick to avenge his innocent blood! We all propose to inquire closely into this crime to prevent you from committing any more atrocities of the sort."

As he said this he left the Queen's presence, but she sent after him to invite him to take a meal with her. He refused. She then begged that, if he would not eat with her, he would at least have a drink, rather than leave the royal household without taking anything. For this he stopped. He was given a glass and swallowed some absinth mixed with wine and honey, which is a favourite drink of the barbarians. It was poisoned. Even as he drank it he felt a great pain in his chest, as if he were being stabbed inside. "Fly!" he shouted to his companions. "Fly, miserable wretches from this horror lest you all perish with me!." They refused to drink and fled at full speed.

As for him, his eyes went blank, he clambered onto his

---

[1]   Bishop Praetextatus was murdered on 24 February 586AD

horse, rode for less than half a mile and then fell dead to the ground (*ibid.*, p. 464).

An inquiry was instituted as despite the Queen's vehement denials King Guntram felt obliged to look into the matter. He sent three Bishops to confer with "the men who were bringing up Lothar" (*ibid.*).

These men are not named although Gregory gives us the names of the bishops, nor it seems are they Guntram's men. They are previously referred to in a speech by Guntram in which he complained that he was not being allowed to see his new nephew.

"When my brother Chilperic died", he said,

> he is reported to have left behind a son. At the mother's behest, those in charge of bringing up the boy asked me to receive him from the sacred font on Christmas Day. They did not come. They made a second proposal, that he should be baptized on Easter Sunday. On that occasion too, he was not produced. Then they made a third suggestion, that he should be presented on St John's Day. Once again, he was not there. Now they have obliged me to leave my home in the sultry season. I have come but the boy is still kept hidden from me and I do not see him (*ibid.*, p. 464).

That the by now year-old prince is in the care of men suggests that they were monks. Could these unnamed men be our Irish monks? It is quite possible that in this atmosphere of bad blood and distrust these foreign monks, who were not implicated in any kind of blood feud, were entrusted with the safety of the young prince. It would explain how it was that Columbanus came to be regarded as a trusted confidential adviser to the Frankish royal family and account for the close relationship he later had with Lothar II who appears to have looked upon him as a father figure.

If so we must slightly amend our time-line as Guntram is clearly making his complaint in July (the dog-days or sultry season—St John's Day is midsummer's eve, 24th June). This would suggest work on the foundation at Anagrates cannot have started much before the end of the summer of 585 AD which might explain why they had such difficulty getting it going.

Having despatched one enemy Fredegund then sent assassins to dispose of Guntram (*ibid.*, pp. 475, 482), Brunhild and Childebert (*ibid.*, p. 489). None of them suceeded but her determination to exact a blood-price for Chilperic suggests that she was not his murderer, although of course it might easily be argued that these assassination attempts were undertaken more in self-defence. She certainly made strenuous efforts to shift the blame. Gregory reports that

> The rumour ran throughout the entire country that Bishop Praetextatus had been murdered by Fredegund, and so she tried to clear herself of the charge by ordering one of her servants to be seized and beaten. "It is you who have brought this infamous charge upon me", said she with great vehemence, "for it was you who attacked Praetextatus, Bishop of Rouen, with your sword."
>
> She handed the man over to the Bishop's nephew, and when he was put to the torture he admitted everything. "I received a hundred golden pieces from Queen Fredegund for what I did," he said. "From Bishop Melantius I received another fifty and from the archdeacon of the city fifty more. In addition to this I had a promise from them that I should be given my freedom and that my wife too should be freed."
>
> As soon as he heard this Bishop Praetextatus' nephew drew his sword and cut the accused man to pieces.
>
> Fredegund appointed Melantius to the cathedral, the candidate whom she had proposed in the first place. (*ibid.*, p. 473).

However, there is one point we should note about her last assassination attempt on Childebert.

Gregory reports her instructions to the assassins:

> Take these two poignards and make your way with all speed to King Childebert, pretending that you are mendicants. As soon as you have cast yourself at his feet, as if you have come to beg for alms, stab him on both sides…

By 'mendicants' is she referring to the wandering Irish monks? This is the only direct reference in Gregory we can find to them despite the fact that they were very active during the period he was writing the book. It is perhaps telling that this one reference is inferring that their activities might have been regarded as a cover for political assassination.

One useful thing we can deduce from this is that the Irish brothers were welcome at Childebert's court and he felt no need to fear them, but then Chilperic too had no reason to fear his assassin.

It looks as if Columbanus and his party had unwittingly stumbled into a nest of vipers and were in great danger of being implicated one way or another in conspiracy and murder. The reason we should be rather cautious about following Gregory's rather obvious trail of clues pointing to Fredegund is that there was a second conspiracy and one in which he and his fellow bishops were clearly implicated.

Immediately following Chilperic's death Guntram ordered an investigation. In the manner of official investigations nothing very definite seems to have come out of it or at least nothing that led to formal charges. Nevertheless Guntram must have found out something because he was stalwart in his defence of Fredegund, who whatever her faults could at least claim that she was now the mother of a king and therefore deserved protection, and firmly declared that he did not believe she was the person responsible.

Instead he laid the blame at another source entirely.

While acknowledging that there were differences within the royal family — adding casually and rather splendidly as an afterthought that "it is true his [Childebert's] mother Brunhild threatened to murder me, but as far as I am concerned that is a matter of small moment" (*ibid.*, p. 437) — he went on, in Bishop Gregory's presence to point the finger at Bishop Theodore of Marseilles who was at that point in exile.

"I am well aware", said Guntram, "that it was he who had my brother Chilperic murdered, and that he did it in collusion with these men" (*ibid.*).

"These men" were the pretender Gundovald and generals Desiderius and Mummolus, both Roman patricians.

Meanwhile when Rigunth found herself on the Spanish border with all the treasure she must have seen her future in clover. Unfortunately she was accompanied by Desiderius. As soon as news reached them that the King was dead he promptly shut Rigunth up in a tower and made off with the treasure to Gundovald.

This, Gregory tells us, was part of a plan that had been hatched two years previously with Mummolus and Bishop Theodore.

In 583 AD the pretender Gundovald had returned to Gaul having spent many years in exile in Constantinople. He returned with a great deal of money. In the same year the Emperor Tiberius II died and was replaced by the Emperor Maurice.

Maurice understandably saw in the fractious wrangling of the Frankish kings a great opportunity for the Roman Empire to re-establish itself in the west. Neither Guntram nor Chilperic at this point had an heir so everything rested on Childebert who was just reaching his age of majority. One of his first acts therefore was to offer Childebert the huge sum of 50,000 gold pieces in return for which Childebert was to have launched an invasion against the Lombards in Northern Italy who threatened the security of the Emperor's Italian capital, Ravenna.

Childebert took the money but then prevaricated. With this kind of money in his treasury his position was secure.

Nevertheless the Emperor had another potential ally in the pretender Gundovald who claimed to be the son of Lothar I. His previous attempt to gain acceptance by the Frankish Royal Family had failed. His supposed father Lothar I had repudiated him. This was unsurprising as he already had four legitimate sons all entitled to a share of his kingdom. He was then repudiated again by Guntram.

Around about this time Guntram was taken very ill and it was thought he might die. Coupled with the enthusiastic attempts on the part of Fredegund to assassinate him it must have seemed an opportune moment for Gundovald to resurrect his claim. Apart from Guntram the only Frankish kings were a 15 year old boy and a four-month old baby.

He recruited Desiderius, general on the side of Chilperic, and Mummolus, who was a general for Guntram, to his cause. Both surnames suggest they were of the Roman senatorial land-owning class. They were backed by Bishop Theodore and, so Guntram strongly hints, Bishop Gregory — in fact probably by all the metropolitan bishops.

Maurice's diplomatic solution is quite clear. With Childebert in his pocket, or so he believed, and the Lombards cleared out of northern Italy, the Empire would re-establish its influence from Sicily in the Mediterranean to what is now the Belgian coast. When Gundovald took over from Chilperic and Guntram the other two kingdoms of Francia the Empire would once again rule through its client kings all of Italy and Gaul. With these central provinces once more under Roman rule it would be a matter of time before the whole of the ancient Empire, East and West, would be re-united.

It's against this background that we must understand Chilperic's need to make alliances with the Visigoths in Lombardy and Spain and his attempt to curb the power of the bishops. He deliberately engineered a conflict between them and the Arians, allowing the state to come down on the side of the latter, and introduced a third party, the Celtic monks, to give them some heavy competition. All his actions in his last years were designed to undermine the power of the metropolitans and the old patrician families who were still amongst the wealthiest landowners in Gaul.

In reading Gregory's account of what happened we therefore have to be very careful about taking him at face value. There can be no doubt that the little bishop was in it up to his neck. Bishop Theodore's arrest and exile resulted from the very specific charge that he had "introduced a foreigner into Gaul with the intention of subjecting a Frankish kingdom to the imperial Rule" (*ibid.*, p. 352).

"They say", adds Gregory, "that he was able to produce a letter signed by all Childebert's principal advisers."

Thus it was that the bishops sought to play off one king against the other, but they were Franks — they were free — and fratricidal though they might have been, they were still family. No matter what they did to each other, nothing compared with the treason of collaborating with the Empire.

Columbanus and his little band of disciples seem to have landed right in the middle of all this. There's no reason to suppose that they wished to get involved.

If they were under suspicion of involvement in either of these conspiracies, even if it were just a case of mistaken identity, they must have been quite relieved to secure a grant of land from Childebert and be able to set out into the secluded forests of the Vosges mountains to search for the abandoned fort of Anagrates where they could turn their backs on the wicked world.

> A wall of forest looms above
> And sweetly the blackbird sings.

goes an early Irish poem.

> And the melodies of chanting birds
> Drift over my books and things (Brown, 2006, p. 98).

How sweet a prospect that must have seemed! How pleasant would be the academic life lived in the wild wood!

Chapter 10

Backwoodsmen

May you have food and raiment and a soft pillow for your
head, and may you be half an hour in heaven before the
Devil knows you're there (Irish blessing).

The Celts lived life quite literally in the round. For them life
was a circle, or more accurately, a series of interconnecting
circles — a spiral with no known beginning and no visible
end.

It is only recently that we have rediscovered the importance of the spiral in our search for the secret of life. The discovery that the conduit of our genetic coding is shaped like
a double helix has once again transformed our world view.
From the strictly rectilinear geometry of modernism artists
and architects are being drawn again to celebrate organic
curves and natural forms.

The Celts — indeed all the people of northern Europe
down to the early mediaeval period — knew instinctively
that the spiral was the key to human existence. The British
and Irish, remember, never did believe that the sun
revolved around the earth. They always knew it was the
other way round and the earth revolves around the sun not
in a perfect circle but in an ellipse. (See further the *Additional
Note* at the end of this chapter, p. 123.)

The Druids were passionate in their belief that the human
and natural world interconnected. The idea of shape-shift-
ing was not so much a belief in a physical reality — no person
has ever been known to actually change species — but a
desire to see the human and animal world as one interconnected whole.

Furthermore they did not exist in a single physical reality.
The story of *The Quest for the Holy Grail* illustrates the sub-

tlety of their mindset. Sometimes the heroes exist in physical reality, sometimes in the Otherworld and sometimes they inhabit a dreamscape which is neither one nor the other.

We find an example of this flexibility of thinking in Jonas' *Life of Columbanus*. Jonas tells us

> While the holy man was wandering through the dark woods and was carrying on his shoulders a book of the Holy Scriptures he happened to be meditating and suddenly it occurred to him to ask himself which he would prefer — to suffer injuries from men or to be torn about by wild beasts. While he pondered earnestly frequently signing himself with the cross on his forehead[1] and reciting prayers he decided that it was better to suffer from the ferocity of wild beasts without sin on their part than from the madness of men who could lose their souls.
>
> As he turned this over in his mind he noticed twelve wolves approaching, some standing to his right and some to his left while he was caught in the middle. He stood still and said "Oh God come to my aid. Oh Lord hasten to help me!"
>
> They came nearer and began to tear at his clothing.
>
> As he stood firm and showed no fear they left him and wandered off into the woods.
>
> Having passed through this hazard in safety he continued on his way through the woods.
>
> Before he had gone very far he heard the voices of many Sueves wandering along the hidden paths. At this time they were very active in robbing travellers in that area.
>
> But by sticking to his path he escaped the danger and avoided misfortune.
>
> Yet he was not clear whether this was some form of delusion or hallucination or whether it had actually happened.

In other words he was not clear if this adventure had occurred in physical reality or while he was "in the Spirit". If the latter we might see it as a useful psychological clue to what he had just been through.

We have already encountered "the interconnectedness of things" in St Patrick's Creed. It was an idea the Celtic

---

[1] This is an interesting link with the "Quest" book in which the knights always make the sign of the cross on their forehead and not across the chest. This reference to Columbanus doing likewise in the sixth century is an important clue to the dating of the book.

Church inherited and Columbanus' insistence that no-one could understand a Creator God without first making a detailed examination of his creation is both a re-statement of the Platonic method of St John and a reflection of his Irish heritage.

This view of the world as a series of concentric circles and interconnecting spirals—which we find graphically depicted in Celtic and Viking art—shaped their physical as well as their intellectual world. Celtic structures were invariably round or elliptical. This applied not only to temple structures like Stonehenge or burial structures like Silbury Hill or Newgrange but also to domestic architecture. The Celtic roundhouse with its thatched roof is still the basis of the "dream house" of most Britons today.

And, getting to the point at last, it was also the dominant form of military architecture. The Celtic hill-fort was round.

We have already noted that Finnian of Clonard and his followers favoured the use of the ancient hill-forts as the best sites on which to found their monasteries.

There were several reasons for this.

One was partly superstitious. In traditional Celtic cosmology the sky-gods were associated with high places and the sea-gods with underground chambers like that at Newgrange.

Along with the high places there are usually associated water-sources, the ubiquitous holy springs or holy wells commemorated in place-names all over the British Isles.

Although some Christians endeavour to avoid a too literal interpretation of the Gospels (e.g. the non-canonical Gospel of Philip, see below p. 170), Jesus Christ might be regarded as a "sky-god" in that the picture language of the New Testament describes him as "ascending into heaven". We have already looked at what John intends us to understand by this process of "ascension" but for centuries artists have represented this process visually by depicting a man rising gracefully into the clouds.

So the early Christian monks, having moved away from the idea of living in total isolation—although as we shall see Columbanus for one didn't abandon the hermit tradition altogether—towards the idea of living in a like-minded community the hill-fort offered an artificially created "telling-place", a "thin" place where traditionally heaven and earth, the physical and spiritual, came into contact and where the "thinness" of the boundary between them facilitated contact.

Again one should not think of this in physical terms but in the sense that it was a place where the meditating monks could achieve a level of transcendant spirituality which would enable them to penetrate what the fourteenth century author called *The Cloud of Unknowing*.

Although the wells on the hill-forts were not holy it is in the nature of military defences that they are sited either with or close to a reliable water supply.

The monastic community needed water for drinking, washing and ritual purposes like baptism.

Last, but not least in such troublesome times, the hill-fort offered a superb defensive position protected by ditch and rampart and usually a wooden palisade along the top of the ramparts and, as we have seen with Inishmurray, sometimes substantial stone walls, with commanding views across the countryside or the sea.

They were built not just to see but to be seen. The early Abbeys were often painted white so that they could be seen for miles. They were literally "White Abbeys". This was certainly true of St Albans.

Whoever commanded the hill-fort was overlord of all the territory round about. Perhaps Finnian had this in mind when he chose the hill-fort for his model.

Henceforth people would look up and see their overlord as not just the High King but the King of Kings, no longer garrisoned by the soldiers of Tara but by the soldiers of Christ.

The hill-fort monasteries were mostly built of wood with a church at the centre and a few communal buildings, a refectory, a guest house, perhaps a hospital or herbarium. There may also have been a library or scriptorium but in the early days the monks probably worked in their cells as we read St Jerome and St Augustine did.

Essentially in its earliest design the monastery was still a hermitage. Some monasteries, notably those of the Carthusians, are still arranged according to this model. The monks only come together for meals and services, otherwise they remain in their cells engaged in solitary prayer and study. This was probably the pattern of life for the Irish monks at the outset although they seem to have regarded hard physical work also as an important part of their daily life and working in the fields and gardens was presumably at least part of the time a communal activity.

When Columbanus took his plan of monastic living to the Continent he copied Finnian's idea of siting his monastery on the foundations of an ancient hill-fort but the hill-forts he had available were not Celtic, they were Roman.

Roman forts were significantly different from their Celtic counterparts. They were, in the same way, all built to a common design, but unlike the Celtic hill-forts the Roman forts were square.

The Roman military distrusted circles. Their world view was almost exclusively conceived in right angles. We have a good example of a Roman hill-fort at Hadrian's wall near Hexham.

Here we can easily see why Columbanus set his sights on this type of building. It was built on stone foundations with good drainage and a water supply. At Hexham there is a bath-house and communal latrines, which might strike us as rather public, but which offered a style of communal living that was far more comfortable and hygienic than that offered by most buildings of the period and perhaps explains why monks had a far better life-expectancy than most people in the Dark Ages. We read that many of them lived to over eighty.

At Caerleon, known to the Romans as Isca, there was a large legionary base. Sixty-four barrack blocks were laid out symmetrically each housing a centuria (80 men). Among other buildings were a granary, a hospital, cookhouses and baths and a latrine with a stone sewer. All the buildings in fact that would be taken over by the monks.

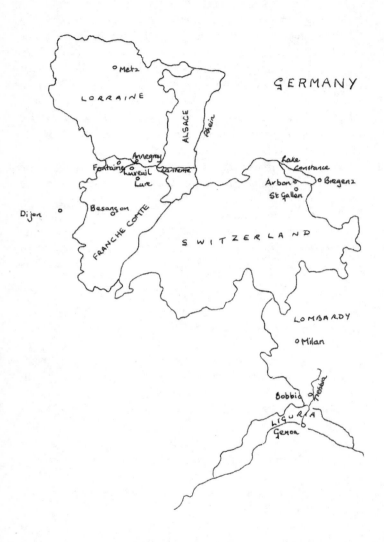

Map showing principal sites associated with
Columban foundations

At Luxeuil we know that Columbanus found thermal springs and the remains of the old Roman baths. He was a tough man but even the hardest men like a bit of comfort now and then. It's not surprising, especially as he was getting older, that he chose to make his home at Luxeuil.

We know that, although the forts had been abandoned since the fall of Rome a century earlier, there must have still been quite a lot still standing. The first thing the monks did on arriving at Anagrates was set about clearing the site and rebuilding the walls.

The tile roofs had probably fallen in and needed to be replaced although often the buildings had thatched roofs even in Roman times. However with the foundations and probably quite a lot of the walls intact the buildings would soon have been brought back into use.

It was this use of the Roman fort that established the monastic pattern of the later Middle Ages, large square enclosures with rectilinear buildings and barrack-like communal dormitories. The circular pattern of the Celtic hill-fort dropped out of use.

At Anagrates they also found a ready-made church in the form of a temple of Diana. If this was still in use[2] they proba-

---

[2] This may well have been the case. Gregory records how one of his colleagues Vulfoliac reported to him how he dealt with the local Diana cult. "I then moved to the neighbourhood of Trier, and on the hillside where you are now standing I built with my own hands the dwelling which you see before you. I found here a statue of Diana, which the credulous locals worshipped as a god. I myself set up a column, on which I remained standing with bare feet, no matter how much it hurt me. When winter came into its season, it so froze me with its icy frost that the bitter cold made my toenails fall off, not once but several times and the rain turned to ice and hung from my beard like the wax which melts from candles. This district is famous for its harsh winters ... All I had to eat and drink was a little bread and green vegetables with some water ... Crowds began to flock to me from the manors in the region, and I kept telling them that Diana was powerless, that her statues were useless, and that the rites which they practised were vain and empty. I made it clear that the incantations which they chanted when they were drunk and in the midst of their debaucheries were quite unworthy of them. Instead they should make a seemly offering of worship to God Almighty, who had made heaven and earth. Night and day I prayed that the Lord would vouchsafe to cast down the statue and free those people from their

bly did so in the manner later described by Pope Gregory the Great to St Augustine prior to his mission to England in a letter which has been preserved for us by the Venerable Bede.

> I have decided [he wrote] ... that the idol temples of that race should by no means be destroyed, but only the idols in them. Take holy water and sprinkle it in these shrines, build altars and place relics in them. For if the shrines are well-built, it is essential that they should be changed from the worship of devils to the service of the true God. When this people see that their shrines are not destroyed they will be able to banish error from their hearts and be more ready to come to the places they are familiar with, but now recognising and worshipping the true God. And because they are in the habit of slaughtering many cattle as sacrifices to devils some solemnity ought to be given in exchange for this. So on the day of the dedication or the festivals of the holy martyrs, whose relics are deposited there, let them make themselves huts from the branches of trees around the churches that have been converted from shrines, and let them celebrate the solemnity with religious feasts ... Thus, while some outward rejoicings are preserved, they will be able more easily to share in inward rejoicing (Colgrave, 1999, p. 57).

For, said Gregory, as in the Old Testament it is the outward deeds that are observed, so in the New Testament careful heed is paid not so much to what is done outwardly as to what is thought inwardly. Things are not to be loved for the sake of a place but places are to be loved for the sake of the good things in them.

This sounds very like Columbanus whose combination of a tolerant spirituality and shrewd appreciation of those things the native population would not give up—like the excuse for a holiday—had in the preceding years resulted in the outstanding success of his mission.

The Celtic foundations quickly attracted applicants.

---

false idolatry. God in his mercy moved their rustic minds, with the result that they began to listen to what I had to say, to forsake their images and to follow the Lord. Then I called an assembly of some of their number and with their help I was able to destroy it myself." This is a useful illustration of how Gregory the Great's policy of working alongside the pagans and then gradually winning them over worked in practice (Thorpe, 1974, p. 446).

One reason for their popularity must have been the fact that Gaul was suffering an unprecedented period of famine followed by sweeping epidemics of plague and dysentery.

Jonas gives the story a somewhat miraculous gloss suggesting that they nearly starved in the first few days after their arrival at Anagrates, having only herbs, bark and the roots of trees to live on. It seems unlikely, having planned the expedition so carefully, that Columbanus would have set out without any provisions at all, but to some extent mendicant monks depended on the generosity of the local population and in a time of famine the local people probably had very little to give.

They were rescued by a local farmer who sent them over a cartload of bread and vegetables in return for their prayers for the recovery of his sick wife. The arrival of these provisions just when things were looking desperate seemed like an answer to their own prayers.

Caramtoc (a Celt himself from his name), the Abbot of Saulcy, sent over a load of bread and vegetables with his steward which helped them through their next thin patch. His intervention is worth noting as it is self-evident that the Irish brothers were not the first to build a monastery in the area. They were in a region where there was a friendly Celtic population and already at least one other monastic foundation.

Jonas tells us the Abbey of Saulcy was a day's journey away through some rough terrain but the fact that they were in contact with the Abbey and also with local farmers suggests that the monks had not cut themselves off from the world, indeed it would rather defeat their purpose if they had done.

The one remaining feature of a Roman hill-fort that I haven't mentioned is the road system. Roman forts were served by Roman roads. At the time of the founding of Anagrates evidently the road was well overgrown since Marculf, the Abbot's steward, had some difficulty finding his way through the woods and had to rely on the good sense of his horses, but in time the monks were able to clear the roads and create a trio of establishments with good communications between them and the outside world which allowed their many pupils and those wishing to enter the religious life to beat a steady path to their door.

Luxeuil was eight miles to the west of Anagrates, probably a larger site since it had hot springs and thermal baths, although these lay stagnant among its pillars. Fontaine—a place that also had hot springs from its name, certainly a reliable water supply—was established three miles north of Luxeuil.

For privacy and to preserve the anchorite tradition of the order, Columbanus found for himself a cave four hundred feet above the valley floor of the River Breuchin.

When he found the cave it was occupied by a bear. "Leave this place", he told the bear, a bit unfairly it has to be said, "and never return".

The bear naturally knew it was being spoken to by a saint and did as it was told.

We can take this story, like the one describing his encounter with the wolves, with a pinch of salt, not only because stories like this occur in almost every saint's life of the period in some form or another, but also because, as we have already seen, at least in the case of the wolves and the brigands, Columbanus himself was not entirely sure that the incident had actually occurred. They are perhaps more revealing psychologically than historically. Yet Columbanus did have a cave which Cardinal Tomas O'Fiaich describes:

> … at the further end of the village [of *Ste-Marie-en-Chanois*—St Mary's in the Oakwood] a path on the left (requiring about half an hour) leads up the hillside to the chapel, cave and holy well of St Columban.
>
> This is the spot traditionally pointed out as the retreat to which the saint used to retire periodically to be alone with God. The bilberry plant which grows wild along the path is still called the *brin bleu de St Columban* and local tradition recalls that when weak with long periods of fasting he was restored by eating the crimson berries. The path finally leads to a ravine, and there one can see the remote cave surrounded by rocks which served as the saint's cell (1990, pp. 110–11).

There is a story too attached to the holy well. St Columban's *minister* — a sort of private secretary or *aide-de-camp* — was a young man named Domoal. Bearing in mind the cave was four hundred feet up from the valley floor he got a bit fed up of carrying water up from the river.

Columbanus, always quite receptive to the grumbles of the faithful, advised him to strike the rock adjacent to the cell whereupon Jonas tells us miraculously the water gushed forth creating the holy well (Jonas, p. 9).

In a more naturalistic light we should remember that Columbanus was a keen observer of natural phenomena and had perhaps noticed that the rock leaked water and deduced that a spring lay behind it.

However it's nice to think that Domoal was thereafter spared the slog up the hill with a bucket.

Here in the quiet of the woods we find the world of the Irish poet — words perhaps copied from those of Columbanus himself — who enjoyed a peaceful studious life accompanied only by birdsong (see p. 112 above).

Additional Note

There is much room for discussion on early cosmologies and the dating of Easter. The principal sources are the works of Martin Brennan ("The Boyne Valley Vision" and "The Stars and the Stones") and Anthony Murphy who have done much research into the monuments of the Boyne Valley — Newgrange, Dowth and Knowth which they believe, like Stonehenge, are ancient astronomical observatories and not just passage-graves.

Their conclusions are necessarily speculative, given the age of the monuments, but they have produced an impressive array of astronomical calculations to back up their claims and their arguments are very persuasive. Most archaeologists are now coming round to their point of view.

Despite the controversial nature of the claim I think it is one worth making here, as it seems to have a bearing on Columban's views, particularly with regard to the dispute concerning the dating of Easter which I discuss in more detail in Chapter 12. Columban insists that the dating should derive from a set of astronomical calculations in the keeping of the monastery at Bangor which it was claimed derived in turn from the work of a "certain Greek". This is possibly either Anatolius,[3] whom he mentions by name, or Meton, a 5th century Athenian who gave his name to the Metonic Cycle, the 19-year lunar calendar which is the basis for the Church Lunar Calendar (see the *Catholic Encyclopedia* entry "The Church Lunar Calendar"). However there is another candidate for the "certain Greek".

Columban's defence comes across as very druidical. The druids self-evidently believed in a sun-centred solar system because theologically they put the sun, the source of light and therefore goodness, at the centre of everything. It appears this may not have been purely symbolic but based on long-standing astronomical observations.

He writes in a letter to Pope Gregory (600AD):

> For the twenty-first or twenty-second moon is *outside the jurisdiction of light* since at that point of time it has arisen after the middle of the night and *with darkness prevailing over light it is illegal … for the festival of light to be held* (trans. G.S.M. Walker, Cork University website; my italics).

But there is more to his argument than the simple symbolic significance of light and darkness representing good and evil.

The Church in Rome and the Eastern Empire followed in the footsteps of 5th century philosophers like Hypatia and the immensely influential Boethius, whose Latin translation

---

[3] Anatolius of Laodicea, the 3rd century Bishop of Laodicea in Syria also known as Anatolius of Alexandria where he was born. He was one of the foremost scholars of his day in the physical sciences as well as in Aristotelean philosophy and is credited with a rich knowledge of arithmetic, geometry, physics, rhetoric, dialectic and astronomy. Eusebius notes "For his learning, secular education and philosophy [he] had attained the first place among our most illustrious contemporaries." He was the author of a treatise on the date of Easter *The Canons of Anatolius on the Pascha* (now lost). Eusebius quotes several paragraphs that display Anatolius' grasp of astronomy in the discussion of the position of the sun and moon in the zodiac at the time of Easter. (*Complete Dictionary of Scientific Biography: Anatolius of Alexandria* — internet edition 2008)

of Ptolemy's work came to dominate the intellectual mainstream in eastern and southern Europe right down to the Reformation, and favoured the earth-centred model of the solar system. This had been described in Ptolemy's *Almagest* to which they stuck until Galileo challenged the accuracy of this model using his own calculations and observations. Even then they were reluctant to accept his findings. Will Durant observes:

> The immense authority of the oft-translated *Almagest* petrified the astronomy of Christian Europe into the Ptolemaic theory of eccentrics and epicycles with the earth at the hub of the world....[4] Another notion of Heracleides, that Mercury and Venus revolve about the sun, had been handed down by Macrobius and Martianus Capella; *John Scottus Eriugena had seized upon it in the eighth century and had extended it to Mars and Jupiter* (Durant, 1950, p. 991; my italics).

Heracleides Ponticus was a "certain Greek" who lived four centuries before Christ and was responsible for several theories relating to the concept of a sun-centred solar system. Possibly he was the Greek Columbanus refers to in his letter to the Pope.

John Scottus Eriugena was another wandering Irish monk of the ninth rather than the eighth century. He wrote two commentaries c 840 and c 850 on Martianus Capella's work *De Nuptiis Philologiae et Mercurii*. According to D. Moran (*Stanford Encyclopedia of Philosophy* 2004):

> The Martianus' commentary [is] most famous for its apparent espousal of a non-Ptolemaic account of the movement of the planets in Book Seven on astronomy. Pierre Duhem thought that Eriugena was offering a version of the system later proposed by Tycho Brahe and in fact Eriugena is correctly reporting Martianus' account which seems to be a version of Heracleides of Pontus' theory.

The eagerness with which he seized upon this theory is consistent with the idea that he came from a tradition which acknowledged the fact that we live in a heliocentric system. His championship of this theory follows the long dispute between the Celtic Church and the Roman Catholic Church

---

[4]   I think here he means the solar system since the earth is the world.

and goes some way to explain why the rift was so bitter and so deep. Although John Scottus is writing two hundred years after Columbanus, there are such similarities in the arguments put forward by the two men that it is clear that they are part of the same tradition: they are both Neoplatonists whose philosophy defines nature as *universitas rerum*, the "totality of all things", an idea inherited by the British Christian Church from the druids. It was this fundamentally distinct intellectual worldview that was at the root of the Easter debate.

Had the argument been solely about the administrative difficulties of reconciling the date of the Easter festival, as is usually argued, the Celtic Church seems to have been unreasonably stubborn and difficult. Iona refused to accept the ruling of Whitby until 716 AD and the Welsh resisted it for a hundred years. If, however, the implication of the new mathematics was to shift from a heliocentric view of the solar system to an earth-centred one, the length and bitterness of the dispute becomes more understandable. Consider our reaction today if we were told to change our view of earth's position in the heavens when the weight of evidence is so clearly against an earth-centred view? Columbanus is fiercely stubborn in defending his church's view. He is totally convinced he is right and as it turns out we now know he was.

Unfortunately we no longer have a copy of the book he wrote on the subject,[5] but we can make some deductions as to the direction of his studies. He suggests that Pope Gregory fears "to be stamped as an innovator like Hermagoras" (*Ibid.*)

Although there are several candidates for Hermagoras the most likely one in the context of his argument would be Hermagoras of Temnos, a 1st Century BC Greek rhetorician who taught in Rome and would thus have been well-known to Gregory the Great. Hermagoras was innovative in developing theoretical models and the idea of stasis. His book has

[5]   Letter to the Bishops 603 AD "For, as I have noted in the book giving my answer which I have now sent to you, though it was written three years ago" (O'Fiaich, p. 75).

been lost but a good part of it was incorporated into Cicero's Invention and other later works so some of his ideas have been deduced. Columban's use of Hermagoras as a model for Gregory suggests that the dispute was, in part, related to theoretical models, in this case models of the solar system. The other subject which Hermagoras was innovative in was the study of fallacies. Columban therefore seems by inference to be suggesting that Gregory should be brave in tackling the fallacy of the Ptolemaic earth-centred solar system.

Columban is pointing Gregory towards the mass of evidence produced by Irish scholars that refute the mathematical model now proposed by Bishop Victorius.

> Victorius [he says] has not been accepted by our teachers, by the past scholars of Ireland, by the mathematicians most skilled in reckoning chronology, but has earned ridicule or indulgence rather than authority. *(Letter to the Bishops 603 AD*, G.S.M. Walker — Cork University website)

Despite his efforts to go on and argue a doctrinal case, it is clear that at the bottom of the dispute is a divergence in the conclusions of the mathematicians. This is fundamentally a scientific argument. Interestingly he contends that the alternative view to Ptolemy was in the ascendant for a hundred and three years prior to Victorius publishing his compilation of the Alexandrian calculations. (*Ibid*)

In his letter to the bishops in 603 AD Columbanus returns to the subject of the dating of Easter which is clearly one of the points on which they are accusing him of unorthodoxy if not heresy. He writes

> I have more confidence in the tradition of my native land, which celebrates Easter in accordance with the teaching and reckoning of eighty-four years and with Anatolius who was commended by Bishop Eusebius, the author of the ecclesiastical history and by Jerome. (*Ibid*)

Jerome, he tells us elsewhere, approved the calculations of Anatolius despite his opposition to him in other matters which appear to have favoured a sun-centred theoretical model. Columban then goes on to refer to "great Martin" which is probably Martianus Capella (rather than St Martin of Tours), whose work was widely reproduced in the sixth century and by Columban's day was effectively a school manual. One of the most important elements in the book was a map of the solar system which provided an alternative to Ptolemy. There is no doubt that the sun is at the centre.[6]

Columban offers an olive branch by declaring the bishops may follow whom they please but throws out the challenge of proof with the quotation "Prove all things, hold what is good." *(Ibid)* He was desperate to air his views in open synod and present all the facts, but he never got the chance.[7]

Although Columban refers to former scholars of Ireland he tactfully refrains from mentioning that many of them were druid but from his insistence on the light/dark ratio this was undoubtedly the case. The heliocentric view of the world was one of the contributions the druids made to the Celtic Church which, coupled with the strong influence of Greek philosophy, caused a fundamental divergence of opinion between the Roman Catholic and Celtic Churches. The Roman Catholic espousal of the earth-centred model endured for a thousand years until the Reformation and improved scientific instruments restored the heliocentric model.

---

[6]   You can find this on the internet at ref Brunelleschi.ims.s.fi.it/.../ MartianusCapellaDeNuptiisPhilologiaeEtMercurii

[7]   Perhaps this was as well. More than two centuries later John Scottus Eriugena was condemned for similar views by the then Pope who ordered his work to be destroyed. Thankfully it wasn't.

Chapter 11

Rule and Penitential

Take time to THINK
It is the source of power...
Take time to PLAY
It is the secret of perpetual youth...
Take time to READ
It is the fountain of wisdom...
Take time to PRAY
It is the greatest power on earth...
Take time to LAUGH
It is the music of the soul...
Take time to GIVE
It is too short a day to be selfish
(*Anonymous*)

We have looked in the previous chapter at the physical environment of our monks.

Bearing in mind the famine conditions of Gaul at this time and the comparative comfort that the Roman forts could offer once cleared of debris, with good drainage, hot water and sturdy stone walls to keep out the unpredictable storms that Gregory of Tours tells us kept occurring, it's not surprising that for many young men the prospect of regular, if sparing meals, and a generally well-ordered life with, for the ambitious a high-flying career path for those with exceptional diplomatic and intellectual skills, seemed extremely attractive.

Within a relatively short time the three foundations of Anagrates, Luxeuil and Fontaine had recruited over two hundred monks.

Columbanus was Abbot, overseeing all three. He was assisted by his private secretary Domoal, his *minister*. He also had with him a bishop, one of his Irish monks named

Aedh, who would provide a link between the monastery and the Episcopalian administration that was responsible for the government of the church in Gaul.

Since there were relatively few monasteries in the region (although as we have seen there was at least one other) at this date co-operation with the metropolitan bishops was essential.

The abbot was supported by a group of his most senior monks — the *seniores* — who in later mediaevil times formed the chapter. In the early days these would have been his twelve companions. They advised him in the direction of the community and the training of novices and from their ranks all the official positions within the monastery were recruited.

In addition to the *minister* the Abbot was assisted by the *oeconomus* who, as the name suggests, was the Bursar with charge of the monastery's finances and all their material resources. Additionally there was the master of the guest-house, the cook or cellarer, if there was a hospital or herbarium the monastery's doctor and, once a scriptorium had been established for the copying of manuscripts, a librarian.

The daily fare was, according to Columban's own recommendations in his Rule, such drink as to avoid drunkenness so that it may sustain them and do them no harm (which we may take to indicate water, milk, water mixed with wine and beer).

Jonas tells us a story which confirms this last item which, as with most of his tales of life in Columban's monasteries, he presents as a miracle wrought by the saint illustrating as he does so further evidence that the North–South European divide is of very ancient origin

> When dinner-time came and the cellarer was getting ready to serve out the beer (which is made from boiling down the juice of corn or barley and which, instead of wine which is preferred above all other beverages by all the nations of the world, is the favourite drink of the Scots and the other nations which inhabit the lands bordering the northern ocean, that is Gaul, Britain, Ireland and Germany and those tribes who share their customs) he carried down to the cel-

lar a jar called a *tybrium* and placed it underneath the tap of the barrel which held the beer. Having drawn the bung he allowed the beer to flow into the jar.

Another brother called him and told him the Abbot wanted him. Burning with the fire of obedience he went at once, forgetting to replace the bung (called a *daciculum*). In fact he still had it in his hand when he rushed up to the blessed father.

After he had done what the Abbot wished he rushed back to the cellar thinking that everything would have run out of the barrel where he had left the tap running but when he got there he found all the beer had flowed into the jar and not a single drop overflowed. It seemed as if the jar had doubled in size (Munro, n.d., p. 10).

The aim of this story from Jonas' point of view is to draw a parallel with the story of Jesus turning water into wine and thus confirm the saintliness of the Abbot who has used his spiritual influence to prevent the distress of his cellarer on discovering his mistake. It doesn't seem particularly miraculous since the prosaic might conclude that either there was not as much beer in the barrel as the cellarer assumed or someone else had spotted the overflow and replaced the first jug with another larger one.

However you take these stories they help us to build up a picture of monastic life. It appears that, as in later mediaeval households, beer was the normal accompaniment to a meal.

Additionally, according to the recommendations of Columban's own Rule, they were allowed vegetables, pulses, flour mixed with water (by which he perhaps meant some sort of porridge or a flat bread like oatcakes) along with a small loaf of bread.

However we also know from the bilberry trail near his cave that they ate fruit and they were not entirely vegetarian. Jonas gives us two stories which demonstrate that both fish and fowl made up part of their diet (*ibid.*, pp. 10, 28).

From these details it seems that, periods of extreme asceticism apart, on the whole the monks enjoyed a healthy diet which goes some way to explain why their life expectancy was far greater than average and we read of many of them reaching a ripe old age.

Their relative isolation also helped to protect them from the plague which swept across Europe at fairly frequent intervals at this time.

As well as adopting the Celtic tonsure which we have already mentioned as distinct from the Roman pudding bowl cut, the monks wore sandals and a long white tunic of undyed wool or linen, covered for warmth by a rough woollen cloak with a hood which was brown.

Their daily life consisted of a constant round of prayer, manual labour, study and mortification.

Mortification requires a bit of explanation. This was not simply masochism as we would put it in modern psychological terms. Its purpose was to minimise the demands of the flesh to enable the spirit to approach a condition of purity. In the same way, and as part of the same process, meditation was designed to achieve an "out of body" experience. In a trance-like state the practitioner could achieve a condition of spiritual detachment which allowed a mystical union with, or at least a momentary glimpse of, the non-physical world occupied by the Creator.

Bede, describing the daily life of Pope Gregory the Great, explains how he achieved this mystical experience.

> ... he proceeded to live with such grace and perfection..that his soul was then above all transitory things; and that he rose superior to all things subject to change. He used to think nothing but thoughts of heaven, so that, even though still imprisoned in the body, he was able to pass in contemplation beyond the barriers of the flesh. He loved death, which in the eyes of almost everybody is a punishment, because he held it to be the entrance to life and the reward of his labours (Colgrave, 1999, p. 65).

The fourteenth century book *The Cloud of Unknowing* is a handbook to explain the process of meditation that the monks would have used.

The day would be punctuated by the recitation of the Divine Office at the canonical hours, the night office being the most prolonged being held at a time with fewer distractions.

The hours were the third (terce) at 9.00 am, the sixth (sext) at midday, the ninth (none) at 3.00 p.m., Vespers or Evensong at 6.00 p.m., Midnocht or midnight and Compline at 3.00 a.m. They all remained unchanged throughout the year except Compline which varied with the time of year reaching its maximum of 36 psalms during the long winter nights from 1 November to 1 February, the traditional Irish winter. Saturday and Sunday mornings required a double dose of devotion so that during the winter the monks chanted the whole of the Irish psalter, the *tri chaoga* over these two days (O'Fiaich, 1990, pp. 26–7).

Otherwise the monks were engaged in the usual agricultural pursuits and crafts that would make the monastery self-sufficient.

Those who were not engaged in hard manual labour were encouraged to study and attain a high standard of Latin, also learning at least a smattering of Greek from those who had fled from the East for whom Greek was their first language.

They read all the pagan classical authors and studied the scriptures intensively. Columbanus also directs us to the study of what was formerly called "natural philosophy" and is now called science. This recommendation, coupled with a minute observation of natural phenomena, suggests the development of an embryonic scientific technique.

The other activity for which we have great cause to thank these dedicated men and women was the copying of manuscripts, often from delicate papyrus which would not have survived, on to more long-lasting vellum or parchment, although not, as I have already pointed out, before the late sixth/early seventh centuries. Nevertheless, even while they were still using paper they were responsible for the creation of a network of substantial libraries across the continent.

In this way the knowledge of the ancient world as well as new discoveries in this curious age was preserved and passed down to us.

To concentrate the mind and maintain order the monks were subject to a Rule and Penitential. The one that survives which was written by Columbanus is one of the earliest and most influential.

It has been criticised by modern commentators as being too severe but its similarity to the rule of Finnian at Clonard and that of Comgall at Bangor suggests that in drawing it up Columbanus was not seeking to be particularly original but merely drawing on his own experience.

Before judging it we should also consider the society for which it was designed.

In a tribal society where either the population is nomadic or buildings are made, as they were in sixth century Ireland, of wicker and wattle, long-term imprisonment is not an option.

In the Irish legends the hero Cuchulain, who admittedly has super-human strength, is described as entering the king's palace by simply lifting up the wall. If you envisage the wall as bricks and mortar this seems an idiotic suggestion but if you think of the wall as lightweight woven willow and mud plaster it becomes not only plausible but something a reasonably strong fellow could manage with ease.

A prison built in this fashion wouldn't be likely to hold anyone for very long.

Accordingly in such societies — and one has not only the Irish legal code as an example but also that of Leviticus containing the law of Moses — a legal code is developed which is based on compensation. An elaborate system is worked out defining the precise restitution that is required to atone for each particular offence. It was for this reason that the Irish developed the profession of the *brehon*, a legal expert with an intimate knowledge of the codex and how it should be applied.

We have already seen that the punishment for an illegal death — where not resolved through the blood-feud — was exile, ten years for manslaughter and life for murder.

Lesser crimes were settled by the payment of the prescribed compensation — usually in cattle which represented the highest form of wealth in an agricultural society — by the perpetrator to the victim. There are many agricultural communities around the world where the law is still administered in this fashion.

In a small-scale society where everyone is known to nearly everyone else this works because, in addition to the serious threat of financial loss and livelihood, the system is backed up by a strong set of social sanctions. "Naming and shaming" works very well where everybody knows your name. It works less well in large urban communities where people tend to be strangers outside a very limited social circle.

In the Roman Empire the spread of urbanisation and large mixed communities meant that this type of legal system no longer fitted the bill and Roman Law, like modern European law, began to rely more and more on physical punishment (torture, flogging and execution as well as long-term imprisonment and hard labour either in dungeons or as galley-slaves) as the basis of their penal code.

The monks in the Vosges mountains however had moved, if not beyond the reach of the law, at least out of its immediate grasp, and so they were able to devise their own system of punishment, the Penitential.

Since monks by definition own no property the principle of material compensation fell short. The Penitential, while keeping the principle of the Irish legal code that for every offence there is a corresponding price to be paid, had to substitute property with pain.

Hence nearly all the punishments in the list designed for monks involve blows to the palm with a leather strap although for lesser offences minor penances like fasting, silence or long periods of prayer with arms outstretched for maximum discomfort were substituted.

Tomas O'Fiach observes:

> The Rule is strict in its demands but its tone is balanced and tolerant throughout. With the exception of one long chapter laying down regulations for the recitation of the Divine Office and some prescriptions regarding food and drink the Rule is exclusively concerned with the dispositions of the soul. In this Columban's Rule differed enormously from the detailed regulations laid down in the Rule of St Benedict (1990, p. 66).

And when examining the Rule and Penitential we must always keep in mind the fact that this is a voluntary code. The monks would, up to a point anyway, welcome correction as a means of improving their spiritual welfare and enhancing their chances of making progress along the path to enlightenment and perfection.

The whole reason for being a sixth century Christian monk was to become a perfect man and thus Christ. To this end they would undertake the most exacting trials. The object of the Rule and Penitential was, while catering for this need, to ensure that the desire for the mortification of the flesh did not go beyond bounds.

It also gives us an insight into the priorities of the brotherhood. Being argumentative might be dealt with by the relatively minor imposition of silence. The most serious corporal punishment is reserved for those who fail to perform the Divine Office correctly or behave disrespectfully during these most sacred hours.

All the same the robust common sense that runs all through the Rule recognises that human weakness is not always something under our control. Bursting out laughing during prayers deserves a "grave penance" but Columbanus, who was clearly a man with a sense of humour, adds prudently "unless it happens excusably."

Sometimes, even in the most sacred moments, funny things happen and you just can't help laughing.

The penitential is split into three sections, for the monks, for the secular clergy and for the lay brothers. When we come to the lay brothers we are back in the realm of the Irish civil code we met at the beginning.

"If any layman commits theft", for instance, "that is, steals an ox or a horse or a sheep or any beast of his neighbours, he must first restore to his neighbour the loss which he has caused" (*ibid.*, pp. 68–71).

One proviso he makes which we might usefully consider, given that gluttony and obesity are the besetting sins of our times, is that "if any layman becomes drunk or eats and drinks to the point of vomiting, let him do penance for a week on bread and water."

Regulating someone's diet would have been fairly easy where all meals were taken communally and perhaps it could be applied conveniently to school dinners.

For more serious crimes the penalties were carefully constructed to allow for gradual rehabilitation as well as restitution.

For perjury, particularly in a case where someone accepted payment to slander another — slander being a serious matter in a society where reputation and honour were almost beyond price — the penalty is set out in stages.

First, three years exile, unarmed, living on bread and water. In a forest populated with bears and wolves, never mind predators of a more human kind, this would put the perpetrator in a very precarious position.

Assuming he survived (and of course assuming he is a he) for the next two years he may return to life in the community but must continue to observe dietary restrictions abstaining from wine and meat. In order to repair the damage he has done he is then allowed to offer "a life for himself" by freeing a slave or bondservant from a life of servitude — giving them back their life in return for his own[1] — and he must give alms frequently.

Having thus been forced into atoning for his bad behaviour with good deeds, he is allowed to eat anything he likes except meat and so is gradually over a seven year period admitted back into polite society.

Similarly if a man sheds blood and by wounding his neighbour puts him out of work, if he can't pay to restore the damage, he must do his neighbour's work for him as long as he is sick and send for a doctor to care for him.

This common sense approach was lifted from the native legal code of the tribal people of northern Europe. Practical and humane, it is, like the penitential set out for the monks, intended to compensate and rehabilitate, correct rather than punish, bringing the straying sheep back to the fold and, in

---

[1]   The monastic equivalent of this is illustrated in the story of St Molaisse exhorting Columba (whichever one is intended) to save three thousand souls to expiate for the war dead.

the case of laymen, direct them once more along the path of civil rectitude.

Of recent years our justice system having traditionally been modelled on Roman jurisprudence with its emphasis on physical punishment and imprisonment has become top-heavy with a prison population spiralling out of control. As a result it has become necessary to look at other ways of dealing with offenders.

Columbanus designed his penitential on the principle that every wrong-doing should be corrected by emphasising its opposing virtue. Thus the talkative or argumentative should be reproved by silence, the restless forced to practice patience, the gluttonous made to fast and so on.

It was not so much a system of punishment as re-training. In that, as with so many things, he was a man well ahead of his time.

Chapter 12

The Perfect Diplomat

By 593 AD work on the three monasteries at Anagrates, Luxeuil and Fontaine had been completed and recruits were already flocking to them.

Most of these were Franks, although they may have been joined by a few more Irishmen and Britons as the first great wave of European missionary work to the lands east of the Rhine got under way.

Their principal asset was their scholarship. Bede tells us of one of Columban's protogées, the Abbess Fara, who founded a monastery (presumably a double house not just a convent) at Brie:

> At that time [i.e. around the year 640 AD] because there were not yet many monasteries founded in England, numbers of people from Britain used to enter the monasteries of the Franks or Gauls to practise the monastic life; they also sent their daughters to be taught in them and to be wedded to the heavenly bridegroom. They mostly went to the monasteries at Brie, Chelles and Andeleys-sur-Seine (Colgrave, p. 122).[1]

Fara was nine years old when Columbanus, a friend of her parents, dedicated her to the religious life. So it is not remarkable to find that her monastery is run in the Celtic fashion, nor is it remarkable to discover that the main attraction of life in these monasteries was the education they offered. What is remarkable is that twenty-five years after Columbanus' death the Anglo-Saxon kings and nobility, despite the best efforts of the Roman church to recruit them to its cause, still preferred to educate their children in the

---

[1] The monastery was strictly speaking called Faremoutier (after the Abbess Fara)-en-Brie.

Celtic tradition. Truly the land of the Angles had become England.

By 592 AD then the fame of the Irish scholars was spreading across the Continent and if Gregory and his fellow bishops had hoped they would disappear into the wild woods never to be seen again they were sorely disappointed.

It was at this time that Gregory of Tours began his remarkable work *The History of the Franks* without which we should know hardly anything about this period and for that he is to be congratulated.

It's a strange book. Gregory insisted that it should not be quoted piecemeal but always entire and begged that it should not be destroyed.

An author's vanity perhaps but, as well as being a useful chronicle of events, it is a work of self-justification. Throughout Gregory, despite his self-deprecation and irony, is the hero of the hour, defending the church against heretics with great courage, ministering to his flock with true Christian charity and in every way living up to his own self-image as a noble Roman from a senatorial family.

On the other hand he offers so many red herrings and motives that it becomes clear that he is anxious to throw us off the scent in the matter of who was responsible for the death of King Chilperic.

Were it to be established that the King, however unpopular he might have been at the time, had died as a result of a conspiracy of the bishops (possibly through collusion with the Roman Empire), it would not have gone down well with the Frankish nobility.

Far from enhancing the chances of rebuilding the Roman Empire through the good offices of the Church of Rome it would probably have had the opposite effect and driven them into the arms of the other churches. The news that the Celtic Church through the energy and zeal of its missionary monks was gaining daily in popularity must have filled Gregory with foreboding.

Then there was always the possibility that the Irish monks knew something of the affair that now they were returning to the world they might choose to reveal.

Gregory had another reason for wanting to put his side of the story. Guntram, who had protected him if only for his own reasons, died in 593 AD and had perhaps been ailing in the previous year. He had suffered from gout in 591 AD which had nearly prevented him from attending his nephew Lothar's baptism.

Childebert II was now king of both Austrasia and Burgundy and as the only surviving adult male of the family he must also have taken over the guardianship of Lothar giving him *de facto* control over the whole of Francia.

Although Gregory had always been extremely loyal to the house of Sigibert he must have noticed with growing unease the good relationship that was building up between the Irish Abbot, the Queen Mother Brunhild and the young king.

However he did not have time to worry about it for long because in the year 594 AD he died and we lose one of our most valuable insights into the period.

Childebert died the year after in 595 AD and Francia which had been briefly reunited under his overlordship was again divided into three.

Lothar, then aged eleven, was heir to Chilperic's kingdom of Neustria.

Childebert had two sons. The eldest Theodebert was ten years old. The chronicle of Fredegar reports that he was the son of a concubine and rather scurrilously suggests that his father was one of Childebert's gardeners and he therefore had no royal blood at all. I think we can discount this as a late piece of propaganda. Gregory makes no mention of any such rumour at the time of his birth only that Guntram received the news with great pleasure. The fact that Childebert divided the kingdom fairly between his two sons and that Theodebert, as the eldest, inherited his own kingdom of Austrasia, indicates that as far as everyone was concerned he was legitimate.

It seems probable that Childebert, following the practice of his uncles had two wives. His second wife, Queen Faileuba, was the mother of his second son Theoderic. It's possible that Theodebert's mother, who is not named, died in childbirth and Childebert then remarried, observing the Christian practice of monogamy like his father, but as Theoderic was only a year younger than his half-brother it seems quite likely that Childebert had two wives at the same time.

Theoderic, as the younger brother, inherited the kingdom of Burgundy, the predominantly southern kingdom that had been controlled by King Guntram. However we must always bear in mind that these kingdoms were not separate nation states and it appears that Anagrates, Luxeuil and Fontaine, although they had originally been in the jurisdiction of Austrasia when Childebert inherited that kingdom from his father Sigibert, at some time or other had passed into the ownership of the King of Burgundy so that Theoderic was now their overlord.

In 595 AD he was only nine years old and the whole kingdom of Francia, with all three kings under age, was in a precarious position.

They needed a guardian. The two Queen Mothers Fredegund and Brunhild were barred from acting as regents by Salic law. It is often assumed that they acted as regents in the manner of later mediaeval queens but as we saw in the case of Childebert and Lothar it was Guntram as the next male relative who took on the position of guardian so this cannot have been permitted.

As they had to have a male guardian it is likely that the role fell to Columbanus.

By way of comparison, a century later in 704 AD, King Eadwulf of Kent died after only a two-month reign and was succeeded by the son of King Aldrith, a boy named Osred who was only eight years old. In the absence of an adult regent St Wilfred adopted him as his son. In doing so he was possibly following an already well-established precedent (Deansley, 1961, p. 100).

The Irish Abbot was much respected for his scholarship and integrity. Since he was devoted to the monastic life he had no worldly ambition and no interest in material rewards. Such a man was entirely incorruptible.

As a Celtic Christian he was regarded as orthodox in his acceptance of the Trinity — indeed the Celts with their love of triads were more passionate about the Trinity than anyone — and his acknowledgement of the leadership of the Pope. This made him acceptable to the Roman bishops.

As a Celt he was also inclined to free-thinking and sufficiently independent fom Roman influence to be equally acceptable to the Frankish nobility.

Jonas tells us that after the foundation of Luxeuil

> ... people streamed in from all points of the compass in order to consecrate themselves to the practice of [the Christian] religion so that in a short time there was so large a number of monks they scarcely all had sufficient room.
>
> The children of the nobility from the areas all around strove to come hither despising and spurning the trappings of the worldly pomp of the wealth of this life. Instead they sought eternal rewards (Jonas, p. 9).

If Luxeuil was fast becoming the Eton of the day it is very likely Columbanus was given charge of the education of the boy kings and perhaps even adopted them as his own sons as Wilfred later did Osred, which would account for the strong influence he had over them thereafter.

He was also, as a (by now fairly elderly at fifty-two) celibate monk, a man who could hold the ring between the two warring Queen Mothers without being accused of susceptibility to either.

The arrangement appears to have worked well since he was held in affection by both Lothar and Theodebert to the end of his life although he clashed with Theoderic as we shall soon see.

His period of guardianship was fairly short since Lothar was nearly of age — twelve being the age of majority for the Franks — and Theodebert and Theoderic were not far off, but having regard to their youth he continued to exert a considerable influence over them for some years after.

This influence must have set alarm bells ringing in Rome. Pope Gregory was a tolerant and reasonable man but he was a Roman of the old school. He came, like Gregory of Tours, from an old senatorial family and high on his list of priorities was the re-establishment of the Roman Empire—as a cultural if not a political unity—through the good offices of the Roman Catholic Church. One of his arguments against the persecution of the Jews was that they had rights of Roman citizenship.

He had become Pope in 590 AD and in six years he had seen Roman influence crumble. By 596 AD, thanks to the influence of Columbanus, the Celtic Church held sway over all the Frankish kingdoms—that is all of Roman Gaul. Brittany, Ireland and Wales, Cornwall, Scotland and Northern England were also dominated by the Celtic Church. Spain and Northern Italy were Arian. Eastern Italy from Ravenna down to the far south and Sicily was Greek Orthodox. The sphere of influence commanded by the Roman Catholic Church appeared to be rapidly shrinking. The dream of rebuilding the Roman Empire in the west was beginning to fade.

It's against this background that we have to see Augustine's mission to the English. Gregory had toyed with the idea of a similar diplomatic and missionary expedition himself prior to his elevation to the Papal See but events had intervened. He must now have seen this mission as a matter of urgency. If England was lost to the Celtic Church then Rome would have only western Italy as its heartland, a poor shrunken thing compared to Justinian's dream of West and East reunited.

The Anglo-Saxons had principally conquered the south-east of what is now England and East Anglia, as the name suggests, but this was also the heartland of Roman Britain and the area where the Romans could expect to find most support in the native population which must have been largely Romano-British. The Saxons came as overlords. They could not have been that great in numbers, but they married into the local aristocracy and Continental royal families.

Gregory had found a way into the Saxon camp.

King Aethelbert ruled one of the more stable Saxon kingdoms, Kent in the far south-eastern corner of Britain and closest to the continent but his kingdom extended at that

time as far north as the Humber so it included the later kingdoms of East Anglia and Mercia within its boundaries.

Aethelbert had married Ethelburga, usually known in
England as Queen Bertha, who was the daughter of one of
the sons of Lothar I, King Charibert. Like the other
Merovingians she was nominally a Roman Catholic
although Aethelbert was a pagan. It was Bertha who was to
persuade her husband to embrace Christianity as a Roman
Catholic and invite Augustine to Canterbury to begin his
mission.

Augustine's first outing was a disaster. He and his monks
chickened out and returned to Rome. Gregory chivvied him
up and sent him back again and this time he landed with his
companions at Thanet, an island in the Thames estuary.

Here the king met him and gave him permission to continue with his mission but Aethelbert was clearly mindful of
the potential for conflict between the churches not to mention friction with the pagan priesthood that the Saxons had
brought with them.

Bede tells us that although he reluctantly allowed Augustine to continue, and provided him with a base in Canterbury, "he compelled no-one to accept Christianity" because
"he had learned from his teachers and guides in the way of
salvation that the service of Christ was voluntary and ought
not to be compulsory" (Colgrave, 1999, p. 41).

Augustine must have been dismayed to learn that
although the King was amenable to the idea of conversion
to Christianity the Celts had got there first.

In the year 600 AD a degree of animosity had clearly
begun to grow between the Roman and Celtic factions.
Dangerous allegations of heresy were hanging in the air as
the question of the date of Easter reared its ugly head.

The Irish and British churches computed Easter in such a
way that the date of this moveable feast occurred two weeks
earlier than when it was calculated according to the Roman
method.

It is true that this led to some complications at a domestic
level. Bede tells us that where the King was Roman Catholic

and his wife a Celtic Christian he would still be in the middle of Lent when she was celebrating Easter.

On the face of it the dispute had nothing to do with theology but was merely the result of developments in mathematics. In 457 AD Rome favoured the solar cycle calculated by Victor of Aquitaine but by 525 AD they had switched to using that of Dionysius Exiguus, a Syrian monk who lived in Rome but followed the mathematicians of Alexandria.

At St Comgall's Bangor higher mathematics had been studied for the reckoning of the date of Easter. Sinlan Moccu Min, a former abbot of Bangor, was said to be "the first of the Irish who learned the computes by heart" (in a very Druidical manner) from "a certain Greek".[2] Later one of his pupils on Cranny Island in nearby Strangford Lough wrote the calendar down.

We have seen how Columban was familiar not only with his native tradition, but also with the Greek and Latin philosophers who propounded an alternative theory to Ptolemy. It was from their standpoint he was arguing in the Easter debate, but the discrepancy between the old mathematics and the new resulted in confusion all over Europe. In 577 AD Gregory of Tours writes

> In this year there was a dispute about Easter. We in Gaul, in common with many other cities, celebrate the holy feast of April on 18 April. Others have agreed with the Spaniards on keeping the feast on 21 March (Thorpe, 1974, p. 274).

The Church in Rome had made an attempt to standardise the dating. In 541 AD Pope Hilary I asked Bishop Victorius of Aquitaine (not the first Bishop Victor but perhaps a descendant) to draw up the Cursus Paschalis to settle the question. Unfortunately this Victor introduced an even more contentious issue into the mix.

Victorius, says Gregory, "had written that Easter should be celebrated on the fifteenth day after the full moon". To prevent Christians from holding the feast on the same day after the full moon as the Jews, following Victorius' recom-

---

[2] On the uncertain identity of this "certain Greek", widely believed to have been Anatolius of Laodicea, see p. 113 above.

mendations Gregory added: "The Church of Rome cele-
brates on the twenty-second day. ... As a result many
people in Gaul hold Easter on the fifteenth day, but I myself
kept the feast on the twenty-second day."

Gregory is silent on the implied anti-semitism expressed
by Victorius, merely emphasising his own orthodoxy, but
we have seen how a few years later Chilperic used this
aspect of church policy to his own advantage.

At Luxeuil Columbanus had been following the Irish
cycle which he brought with him from Bangor and now
came in for criticism on the grounds that this cycle meant
they periodically celebrated Easter on the same date as the
Jewish Passover.

Columbanus was quite outraged by the implication. "We
ought not to hold Easter with the Jews?" he writes explo-
sively to Pope Gregory the Great in 600 AD. "What rele-
vance has that to reality?"

That this drift to intolerance and anti-semitism got right
up the noses of the Irish is clear from the fact that this row
continued to simmer long after Columbanus had died. In
629 AD the southern Irish accepted the proof of the Alexandrian mathematicians and agreed to accept the Roman dating of Easter but the northern Irish and most specifically
Abbot Segene of Iona stuck to their guns after receiving a
letter from the pope-elect John IV reproving them for their
willingness on occasion to celebrate Easter on the same day
as the Jews. This explains their determined stand at the
synod of Whitby and the refusal of many bishops and
abbots to accept the decision when it went against them.

Columbanus' letter to Gregory the Great also indicates
that in addition to the physical calculation of the solar cycle
there was a symbolic and moral dimension to be taken into
consideration.

The philosophical argument he gives against adopting
the recommendations of Victorius are equally interesting in
that they give us a rare insight into Druid beliefs.

In the same letter Columbanus quotes Anatolius whom
he describes as "a man of envious learning" as arguing concerning Easter that:

Certainly if the moon's rising shall have delayed until the end of two watches, which marks the middle of the night, light does not prevail over darkness but darkness over light, for it is certainly impossible that at Easter some part of darkness should rule over the light, since the festival of the Lord's resurrection is a festival of light and there is no communication of light with darkness. And if the moon has begun to shine in the third watch there is no doubt that the twenty-first or twenty-second moon has arisen on which it is impossible for the true Easter to be celebrated under conditions where darkness rules to some extent. And we also read in the book of sacred dogma: Easter, that is the festival of the Lord's resurrection, cannot be celebrated before the passing of the Spring Equinox the beginning of the fourteenth moon (Gennad De Dogm. Eccl. 87) namely to avoid its preceding the equinox.

This accords with the Druid association of light with goodness and with Columban's assertion that there is no such thing as evil only the absence of good. This follows from the observation that there is no such thing as darkness only the absence of light. Since the absence of light equates to the absence of goodness he is arguing it would be inappropriate to hold Easter, a festival of light, at a time when darkness is in the ascendant.

In this letter however we find Columbanus dealing in the matter characteristically, writing to Gregory the Great diplomatically raising the issue good-humouredly, arguing his case with reference to a wide range of scholars and exerting his usual charm by asking for the loan of some books to allow him to investigate the matter in a proper scholarly fashion.[3]

Gracious peace to you from God our Father and from our Lord Jesus Christ

I wish, Holy Father, (do not think it excessive of me) to ask about Easter, in accordance with that verse of Scripture "Ask your Father and he will show you, your elders and they will tell you..."

When an unworthy man like me writes to an illustrious one like yourself, my insignificance makes applicable to me

---

[3]   It is interesting to note that in this letter Columbanus refers to two of the British influences mentioned earlier — Finnian and Gildas — indicating their importance to his way of thinking

the striking remark which a certain philosopher is said to have once made on seeing a painted harlot. "I do not admire the art but I admire the cheek." Nevertheless I take the liberty of writing to you strengthened by the assurance of the humility with which you undertake your evangelical duties and I attach the reasons for my unease. There is no need to boast of one's scholarship when one writes out of necessity even when one is writing to one's superiors.

I have read your book containing the pastoral rule. It is succinctly expressed, makes comprehensive reference to doctrine and is crammed with much scriptural knowledge. I acknowledge that the work is sweeter than honey to one in need. As I am thirsty for knowledge therefore I beg you, for Christ's sake, to present me with your commentaries on Ezekial which I hear you have composed with consummate skill. I have read six books by Jerome on the subject but he did not expound even half of the matter.

So, if you please, send me something from your lectures delivered in the city. I mean the last things mentioned in your book. Send as well the Song of Songs from that passage in which it says: "I will go to the mountain of myrrh and to the hill of incense", as far as the end. Treat it, I pray, either with others' comments or with your own in brief. In order to expound all the obscurity of Zechariah, reveal his secrets, so that in these matters the blindness of the West may give you thanks. Everyone knows *my demands are pressing, my inquiries wide.*[4] But your resources are also great, for you know well that from a small stock less should be lent and "from a large one more".

Clearly Columbanus is indicating that he is under pressure to find a solution. He goes on apologising for his presumption but making it clear that he does not intend to back down but to fight his corner.

Let charity move you to reply. Don't let the sharpness of this letter keep you from explaining things, since anger explodes into error, and it is my heart's desire to pay you due honour. My part was to challenge, to question, to beg; let yours not be to deny what you have freely received, to bend your talent to the seeker and to give the bread of doctrine according to Christ's command. Peace to you and yours. Please pardon my rashness Holy Father for having written so boldly. I beseech you to pray for me, a most wretched sinner, even once in your holy prayers to our common Lord.

---

[4]   My italics.

He is laying on the compliments with a trowel, but the reference to the sharpness of his tone and anger "exploding" between them gives us some indication as to the bitter conflict that was now simmering between the Romans and their colleagues representing "the West".

He reminds the Pope that the allegiance of the Celtic Church is entirely voluntary — a matter of goodwill — and that they are fellow Christians under a "common Lord".

But his apologies are formal and his self-deprecation false. He is at least as good a scholar as the Pope and he is confident that he can put his case with sufficient force to win the argument.

That is if he is allowed to put it.

We can judge the antagonism that was growing between the Romans and the Celts from two events that occurred in the following year 601 AD.

In the eighteenth century the vicar of the parish of Llangamarch and St David's in Brecknock, the gloriously named Reverend Theophilus Evans, wrote a carefully researched account of the event in Welsh. It has been translated under the title "A View of the Primitive Ages".

He explains the significance of Bangor-Iscoed — "Bangor beside the Woods" — which is neither the Bangor of Comgall in Northern Ireland, nor the Bangor in North Wales which is opposite Angelsey and Holy Island (Holyhead as it is now more generally known where the Irish ferry goes from) but a place on the English/Welsh border about five miles south-east of Wrexham.

> Pelagius received his education at the college of Bangor Iscoed, where he became a monk, and afterwards abbot. This institution may properly be denominated the mother of all learning... In former times there was a very extensive monastery at this place. In addition to the students who were learning the sciences there were 2,400 religious persons who read the service in rotation, a hundred at a time, every hour in the twenty-four, so that the worship of God was continued by day and night throughout the year.

Columbanus instituted in his monasteries the same practice of continual chanting.

We have already met Pelagius. He was the monk named Morgan, another Celtic Abbot who got right up the nose of the Romans. Bangor Iscoed was not just any old monastery, it was the heart of Celtic Christianity in Britain—home of the arch-heretic himself.

Augustine had chosen his target carefully. He had arranged to meet the Britons at a place now called Augustine's Oak (Derwen Austin) on the border of Hereford and Worcester.

However the conference was doomed from the start because of the distrust between the parties. Theophilus Evans tells the story (which is also told in Bede's Ecclesiastical History in almost the same words):

> ... the assembly was held under a thick oak in the open field. A very great number of the Britons attended besides seven of the bishops of Wales viz. The bishops of Worcester and Hereford [then part of Wales] Llandaff, Llanbadarn-fawr, Bangor, St Asaph and Holyhead in Anglesea; besides whom, the able and intelligent students of the college of Caerleon, a place as noted then as Oxford is now, and from North Wales many hundreds of educated teachers from the great monastery of Bangor-is-y-Coed in which were taught at that age all the different branches of literature which were then known for such was the clamour raised by Augustine respecting the supreme authority and claims of the pope that the people crowded from all parts of the country to see the messenger he had sent from Rome. But before they arrived at the end of their journey, some with them met an elderly man, who inquired where they were going.
>
> "We are going", said they, "to meet Augustine who was sent by one he calls the Pope of Rome to preach to the Saxons. He asks us to obey him, and also to receive the same ceremonies and articles of religion as are received and held by the Church of Rome. Pray what is your opinion on this subject? Shall we obey him or should we not?"
>
> The elder answered, "If God has sent him, obey him."
>
> "But how can we know whether he is sent by God or not?" said they.
>
> "By this shall you know", said the elder. "Consider what our Saviour says—'Take my yoke upon you and learn of me, for I am meek and lowly in heart.' (Matt xi 29) and if Augustine is a meek and humble man, and poor in spirit, hear him, if otherwise have nothing to do with him."

"But how shall we know", they rejoined, "whether he is proud or humble?"

"Easily enough", said the elder, "proceed slowly, in order that Augustine may be at the place appointed before you, and sit in his chair. Now he is only one and I am told there are seven bishops on our side, besides many other respectable men, therefore, if Augustine will not rise from his chair and salute you, you may then judge at once that he is a proud man; do not obey him."

The counsel of this elder was considered by the whole of them as a kind warning from God and they were unanimous in adopting it.

Needless to say Augustine did not rise from his chair nor show any mark of respect but displayed all the cold indifference and air of superiority of a proud Roman patrician.

According to Bede he spoke them as follows:

You do many things which are contrary to our customs.[5] Or rather to the customs of the universal church. Nevertheless, if you are willing to submit to me in three points we will gladly tolerate all else you do even though it is contrary to our customs.

These three points were the date of Easter (Bede helpfully explains how the different dates were calculated if you're really interested), to perform the ministry of baptism in the manner practised by the said church and thirdly to assist the Romans in preaching the gospel to the Saxons. Since the Saxons had relatively recently invaded the country this was rubbing salt in the wound.

When the Welsh bishops declined to accept these terms even Bede can hardly believe what happened.

Augustine [he wrote, with barely disguised disgust], that man of God, warned them with threats that if they refused to accept peace from their brethren they would have to accept war from their enemies, and if they would not preach the way of life to the English nation, they would one day suffer the vengeance of death at their hands.

Bede diplomatically suggests this was in the nature of a prophecy and it was through the workings of divine judgement that the Saxon king Aethelfrith attacked Chester.

[5]   Freudian slip. He meant Roman, then realised his mistake and corrected himself.

Before the battle he noticed a great many monks standing apart and was told they had come from the great monastery of Bangor Iscoed "where there were said to be so great a number of monks that, when it was divided into seven parts with superiors over each no division had less than 300 men all of whom were accustomed to live by the labour of their hands" (Colgrave, 1999, p. 76).

We can also guess from the habits of the Irish monks that they practised martial arts, so we should not entirely hold it against Aethelfrith that he ordered them to be attacked first, although the impression we are given by Bede is that he was attacking a contingent of unarmed praying monks.

"It is said", Bede tells us, "that in this battle about twelve hundred men were slain who had come to pray and only fifty escaped by flight."

They were abandoned by their bodyguard led by Brochfael Ysgithrog (Brocmail in Bede) who, to be fair, is reported to have been outnumbered ten to one by the enemy and decided discretion was the better part of valour and withdrew his forces but it is not clear whether when they died they were praying or fighting.

Theophilus Evans assures us they were murdered in cold blood, but as he adds "the papists were then and still remain a vindictive people" we should remember that he was writing in the first half of the eighteenth century when Protestants and Catholics had literally drawn up battle lines. The reverend gentleman was an Anglican vicar so on the Protestant side.

Nevertheless there seems pretty damning evidence that Augustine was implicated in encouraging Aethelfrith to attack the monks of Bangor Iscoed. When he heard what had happened Pope Gregory was appalled. He summoned Augustine back to Gaul and forbade him to undertake missionary work again. He was also alarmed to learn that Augustine had been claiming for himself the power to work miracles. Evidently the man was becoming too big for his boots.

He was replaced by Bishop Laurence (Laurentius) but Laurence it seems was equally shocked by the recalcitrance of the rebellious Celts.

> ... we held the holiness both of the Britons and the Irish in great esteem, thinking that they walked according to the customs of the universal church; but on becoming acquainted with the Britons, we still thought that the Irish would be better. But now we have learned from Bishop Dagan[6] when he came to this island and from Abbot Columban when he came to Gaul that the Irish did not differ from the Britons in their way of life (Colgrave, 1999, pp. 76–7).

The case against Columbanus was hotting up.

He must have been stunned to hear the news of what had happened at Chester and alarmed when he was himself summoned to a synod of the French bishops at Chalon-sur-Saone. This was in 603 AD.

He regarded this situation as so dangerous he declined to attend. He wrote them a letter, still extant, in which he draws their attention to a book he has written explaining why the Irish calculation of Easter is doctrinally correct (this book unfortunately is lost). He mentions it is now three years old and asks that it be allowed to stand for his defence.

He makes again reference to their common Lord, and begs to be allowed to continue to live peacefully at Luxeuil.

> For we are all fellow members of one body, whether Franks or Britons or Irish or whatever our race. Thus let all our races rejoice in knowledge of the faith and in recognising the Son of God. Let us all hasten to approach the perfect manhood...

For the moment the bishops let the matter drop. Columbanus still had the support and protection of all the Frankish kings. Since he declined to walk into the lions' den, the lions could do nothing except growl.

Columbanus had not backed down. He considered that he had put his case and put it well. The Irish monks and

---

[6]   Is this the "soporific sting of Dagon" referred to obliquely in Columban's letter to Pope Gregory of 600 AD who has evidently been arguing "We ought not to hold Easter with the Jews?" Is this a sly pun on his name? Dagon was the god of the Philistines.

their satellite monasteries went on celebrating Easter from the fourteenth to the twentieth day of the lunar month, according to Bede, working on an 84-year solar cycle. That is to say, according to Columbanus, they took the view that the resurrection (i.e. Easter) should not take place before the passion (i.e. the Equinox), and therefore it must end on the twentieth day of the month "lest they should perform a sacrament of the New Testament without the authority of the Old."

Perhaps the silence of the bishops encouraged him to believe he had won, but the truth was they had other fish to fry. In 604 AD Pope Gregory died. He was replaced by Pope Sabinian whose succession may have indicated a change of policy. Sabinian did not live long. He was replaced in 607 AD by Pope Boniface III who had been Gregory's treasurer and with his accession, the Imperial party was once more in the ascendant.

Chapter 13

Shipwreck

You have taken the east from me, you have taken the west
  from me
You have taken what is before me and what is behind me
You have taken the moon, you have taken the sun from me
And my fear is great that you have taken God from me...[1]

The death of Gregory the Great gave Columbanus a little breathing space but he was still in an extremely difficult position, so much so that he wrote at once to the new Pope trying to secure his support without even knowing his name.

In this letter he made another rod for his own back. In order to justify the practice of his monasteries of continuing to observe Easter after the Celtic fashion he drew the Pope's attention to the "hundred and fifty authorities of the Council of Constantinople, who decided that churches of God planted in pagan lands should live by their own laws, as they had been taught by their fathers."

On the basis of this authority he argued that he and his monks "are in their native land as long as we accept no rules of these Franks."

But the monasteries were not strictly speaking "in pagan lands". Although they were on the borders of Burgundy they were still within the territory of a nominally Christian king and in the diocese of a Roman bishop. In advancing his argument that the monasteries were beyond the bounds of their authority Columbanus was pushing his luck.

However he seems to have got the backing of the new Pope whose name as we know turned out to be Sabinian.

---

[1]   From "Donal Og" translated from the Irish by Lady Augusta Gregory.

He also still had the support of Brunhild. The Queen Mother, no doubt acutely aware of the danger her friend was putting himself in, adroitly moved him out of harm's way by sending him on a diplomatic mission to Spain. By this means she removed him physically from the court but at the same time indicated that he still had her complete confidence and was one of her most important advisers.

The occasion of the mission was the proposed marriage of her grandson Theoderic[2] who was nearly nineteen years old and now King of Burgundy in his own right.

Frankish kings were normally married at the age of 15 but Theoderic doesn't appear to have taken a wife, or rather he seems to have chosen one but she was not someone that his family approved of. Since polygamy was normal among the men of the royal family and Guntram and Chilperic both included former servants among their wives the Frankish kings cannot be said to have been at all snobbish. It's unlikely therefore that the objection to Theoderic's mistress was that she was of a lower social class. The objections to the match can only have been on grounds of adultery, if she was already married, or of consanguinuity.

We don't know the name of this mistress. Given that later historians confuse her with the Queen Mother, she may have been another Brunhild, but I find another possibility more likely. Jonas tells us Columbanus exorcised twelve demons at the home of a woman called Theodemanda — indicating an extraordinary concentration of evil in connection with her. The figure twelve — an obvious inversion of the usual twelve apostles — underlines this fact (Jonas, p. 21).

I think it is probable that this Theodemanda was the new Queen of Burgundy (self-styled since she and Theoderic appear to have been unable to marry legally) and that she was the root of Columbanus' troubles there.

The Frankish kings often chose names for their offspring with related prefixes — thus names beginning with Chlo- or

---

[2] Also variously known as Theuderic or Theuderich (French Thierry).

Chlodo abound indicating their descent from Clovis or his son Chlothar (Lothar) I.

The related names Theodebert, Theoderic and Theodemanda suggest a family relationship between the three of them. Theodemanda could therefore have been a half-sister or first cousin of Theoderic which would explain the strong family resistance to their relationship as either way it would have been classed as incestuous under Frankish law. Even if they were not blood relations, but related only by marriage, they would be classed as kinsman and kinswoman and their relationship would still be regarded as taboo.[3]

This would explain the deep disquiet felt by Brunhild and Columbanus about the relationship and the large number of devils required to exorcise the evil influence that appeared to have brought it about.

Whatever the exact nature of their relationship it was clearly felt to be unacceptable. Brunhild set about arranging a diplomatic match for her grandson perhaps in the hope that this would encourage him to break the connection.

Her choice was a Visigothic princess like herself whose name was Ermenburga. Columbanus was sent to Spain to negotiate the marriage settlement and to escort the young lady herself back to Burgundy.

Columbanus was by this time in his late sixties, an old man to be setting out on such a journey, which indicates just how dangerous the situation was that Brunhild felt him to be in.

That he had maintained a close relationship with Theoderic as a boy and was regarded as some sort of father figure is borne out by the fact that Jonas tells us Theoderic

---

[3]　Another possibility is that Theodemanda was the first wife of Childebert and a princess of the Eastern Empire. Names beginning Theo- were common in the imperial family. The Emperor Tiberius II offered to make diplomatic marriages between his daughters and the Emperors Justinian and Maurice Tiberius. It is quite possible therefore that a similar match was arranged for Childebert and their children were Theodebert and Brunhild. However I have not yet managed to trace this princess. Marriages between first cousins and half brothers and sisters were not unknown within the imperial family and it may be that on the Roman side such a diplomatic match might have been more readily accepted.

continued to visit him regularly even after he became king and Columbanus did not waste the opportunity to give him a piece of his mind.

> As he very often visited Columbanus the holy man began to reprove him because he sinned with concubines and did not satisfy himself with the comforts of a lawful wife in order to beget royal children by an honoured queen and not bastards by his concubine.

He duly returned with Ermenburga, mission accomplished, but it was not a success. Theoderic refused to marry the princess and stubbornly maintained his relationship with his mistress, however undesirable his relatives may have regarded it.

Ermenburga, perhaps mindful of what had befallen the unfortunate Galswinth, prudently returned to Spain, but even if she was prepared to swallow the insult patiently Brunhild was not. The simmering conflict between the Queen Mother and her grandson erupted into a blazing row. She walked out of his court and went to live with his brother Theodebert at the Austrasian court.

Whether she walked out in high dudgeon or was ordered out by the woman who had usurped her position (and possibly her name) as Queen we don't know but we can make an educated guess. From this moment on the courts of Austrasia and Burgundy were estranged and in opposition to one another.

In 607 AD Pope Sabinian died and Columbanus was faced with having to come to terms with a new Pope, Boniface III, who seems to have represented the imperial party.

Having sided with Brunhild in the matter of the royal marriage Columbanus now found himself also on the wrong side of the King who controlled the territory on which his monasteries were sited. Matters came to a head in 610 AD when Columbanus was called to the Burgundian court. The King's mistress lined up the two sons she had now produced with Theoderic and asked Columbanus to bless them (Jonas, p. 17). What follows assures us that the King and his Queen were still not legally married despite

appearances because Columbanus refused to give his blessing to their children. This was not on religious grounds-
—after all no child is responsible for its parentage—but for
political reasons.

Theodemanda (if that was indeed her name) was no fool.
If she could not legitimise her position by marrying her
lover then she could seek to do it another way. Guntram had
defended Fredegund on the grounds that "she was the
mother of a king". Theodemanda clearly hoped to shore up
her position as Queen in the same way.

Columbanus was no fool either. He had been for a time
the guardian of Theoderic and perhaps his adopted father.
To be accepted as legitimate a Frankish king had to be publicly acknowledged by the head of the family as Guntram
had done for all his nephews. If Columbanus—standing in
that position in the absence of an older relative—now
publicly gave his blessing to the sons of Theoderic and his
mistress, it might be regarded as legitimising their claim to
the throne and sanctifying an otherwise unholy union.

We can deduce that this was Theodemanda's purpose
because we are told that she presented only two of the four
sons of Theoderic (Lehane, 2005, p. 196). The other two were
the sons of other mistresses and obviously she had no desire
to legitimise them. The two boys she presented were the
children of her own partnership with Theoderic.

In contrast to my reading of the situation, most historians
follow Jonas and the later chronicler Fredegar (who also
uses Jonas as a source) and assume that the Queen on this
occasion was the Queen Mother Brunhild. In consequence
poor Brunhild has come in for a very bad press, being
described quite unfairly as a bloodthirsty tyrant.

This tradition is quite at odds with the description of her
we are given by Gregory of Tours, who knew her well and
admired both her and her husband. He describes a woman
who is well-educated, elegant and gracious, every inch a
queen. Despite considerable provocation and several
attempts on her own life as well as the assassination of her
husband, Gregory offers no example of Brunhild behaving

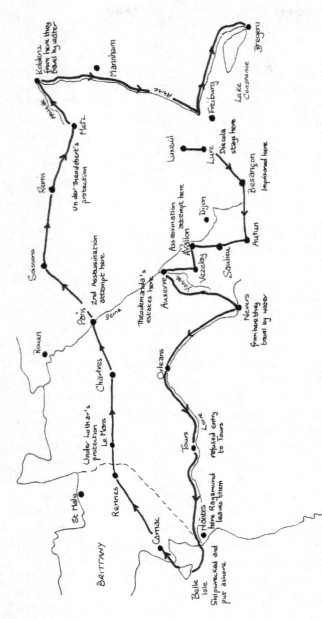

Columbanus' travels across Gaul under safe conduct with Count Ragamund, shipwreck, and return journey to Brigantium [Bregenz].

in a tyrannical or especially bloodthirsty manner. Compared to her in-laws she is a model of restraint.

The "Queen Brunhild" we are offered in these later years is a quite different character: vengeful, spiteful, treacherous, cruel and ambitious. It is possible of course that in her dotage — she was ten years older than Columbanus so was now, if she was still alive, nearly eighty years old, Brunhild had lost her marbles and her personality had undergone a sea-change. However, as we know that she was extremely friendly with Columbanus and had hitherto treated him as a trusted adviser, and had furthermore gone to live with her other grandson Theodebert, I think it is reasonable to assume that here we are looking at a different woman altogether.

Why else should Columbanus have refused to bless the grandchildren of one of his oldest and most faithful supporters?

"You must know", he proclaimed in front of the assembled courtiers, "that these will never hold the royal sceptre because they were begotten in sin" (Jonas, p. 17).

He could not have made it clearer. Even if these were not his exact words, they do at least demonstrate that he had a clear awareness of the political implications of what he was being asked to do. He must have known that his refusal would exacerbate the already tense situation and win the enmity of Theodemanda but there really wasn't anything else he could do.

The "noble and pious lady" (as Jonas once referred to her, probably ironically) was furious. She had lined up her sons very publicly precisely for the purpose of forcing Columbanus into publicly acknowledging them as the king's legitimate sons. His refusal was a slap in the face. If anything happened to Theoderic now the kingdom of Burgundy would be carved up between Lothar II and Theodebert. They remained the legitimate heirs. As a result she stirred Theoderic up against his former mentor.

Orders were issued for a boycott of all the Columban monasteries by the people of the Burgundian countryside. Columbanus appealed against this action to the King over whom he probably still hoped to have some influence. According to Jonas the saint refused to enter the royal palace and smashed the goblets of wine and the bowls of food sent out by the king for his reception (*ibid.*, p. 18). It is more likely that he was refused an audience with the king and his disinclination to taste the food and drink probably had more to do with the suspicion of poison than any righteous indignation he may have felt.

Theoderic at least seems to have proffered some sort of olive branch but it was clearly not in his mistress's interests that there should be any rapprochement between Theoderic and the rest of his family. She continued behind the scenes to urge the need for an investigation of the monasteries and in this she evidently found plenty of support from the bishops.

We can be fairly certain that this was the case because it was in the same year, 610 AD, that Pope Boniface IV, who had come to the Papal throne two years earlier,[4] launched his attack on the Celtic Church.

He wrote to the Irish Church complaining that they were no better (indeed no different) from the Britons with whom Augustine had already had a run-in. The Bishop of London, that Mellitus whom Augustine had consecrated as his deputy when he was recalled from Britain, went to Rome to confer with the Pope about the needs of the English Church. Bede tells us "the holy father had summoned a synod of the Bishops of Italy to draw up regulations concerning monastic life and harmony" (Colgrave, 1999, p. 77).

By the "Bishops of Italy" he means the Romans Columbanus, despite being one of the foremost practitioners of monasticism in Europe at the time, was not invited to attend. Indeed the synod appears to have been held in secret. We only know of it from Bede's account. What it does tell us is that the Pope was intending to bring all the monasteries under his own control and conforming to the Benedictine Rule which was regarded as orthodox and which was, of course, Italian, having started life at Monte Cassino.

---

[4] Boniface III lasted in office less than a year (607 AD).

That they were prepared to put their weight behind Theoderic and his Queen, given the dubious nature of their relationship, is a measure of the desperation felt in Rome.

And elsewhere. In the same year Constantinople saw a political upheaval in which the Emperor Phocas, who had replaced the Emperor Maurice in 602 AD, was himself ousted in a coup and replaced by the new Emperor whose name was Heraclius. Heraclius was a soldier and the Empire was under pressure from the Persians in the East. Eventually he defeated them at Nineveh and re-established the security of the Empire's eastern borders but in 610 AD the situation was much more volatile. Whenever the Byzantines were threatened in the east they looked to expand their territories in the west.

From 610 AD onwards they had good reason to look for political alliances in western Europe. The most vulnerable kingdom and the one most likely to provide them with a fruitful client arrangement was Burgundy. The unpopularity of Theoderic and his mistress, and their isolation from the other kings of Gaul, made them ripe for a diplomatic takeover. By taking them under their wing the Byzantines could stretch their influence in the west from their provincial capital Ravenna right up across Switzerland and well into Gaul. Any loss of territory in the east would be compensated for by the expansion of their influence in the west. At the same time the Emperor was able to put pressure on the relatively new Pope to urge the case for ideological and indirectly political unity between east and west.

In order to achieve this, the first thing Boniface had to do was ensure that the influential and independent Columbanus was removed not only from his abbacy at Luxeuil but from mainland Europe. It's reasonable to suggest that the whole confrontation with Theodemanda was a put-up job. Its outcome was known all along. The objective was to get Columbanus sent back to Ireland.

There is reason to suppose that the Pope had already managed to plant a fifth column at Luxeuil. Some of the Frankish monks who were not as wedded to Celtic practices must have felt that it would be prudent for them to accept the modifications proposed by the new Pope. It seems they were organising a potential coup.

In his letter from Nantes following his expulsion, Columbanus wrote to his friend and replacement

> My dear Attala, you know those who from your point of view are a nuisance. Remove them at once yet get rid of them in peace and agreement with the Rule. If you see dangers come away. The dangers I mean are the dangers of discord. I'm afraid of disagreement there on account of Easter, lest perhaps, through the devil's tricks they may wish to banish you if you do not keep peace with them. Without me you seem to stand more weakly there. Therefore be wary considering "the time when they do not endure sound doctrine".[5] Instruct yourselves and all who may be willing to listen; only let there be none among you who is not united. For you must chiefly strive for peace, "ever anxious to preserve unity of spirit in the bond of peace".[6] What good is it to have a body and not to have a heart?
>
> ...I'm broken I confess for this reason: while I wished to help all, "when I spoke to them they fought against me without cause",[7] and while I trusted all I was almost made a fool (O'Fiaich, 1990, p. 78).

It seems that not all the pressure was from outside the monastery. There were forces working against him from within.

There was at any rate plenty of material to work with. By his penitential discipline, his unauthorised foundations and his independence of action, Columbanus had infringed the authority of the metropolitan bishops. By his calculation of the date of Easter and his persistent adherence to other Celtic habits like the tonsure he opened himself up to charges of unorthodoxy if not heresy.

Added to which his clever defence to the Pope now worked against him. His avowal that his monks remained "in their native land" and took no account of the laws of the Franks put him in clear breach of secular law. He had put himself well and truly on the wrong side of the King.

---

[5]   2 Timothy 4.3
[6]   Ephesians 4.3
[7]   Psalm 109.3

Theoderic was persuaded by his Queen to ride out to Luxeuil and put the question to Columbanus personally (Jonas, p. 18). On arrival he demanded access to all areas of the monastery, which as the King he would normally have expected to have granted. Columbanus explained that outsiders were not allowed within the monastery itself. A guesthouse was provided for their entertainment for this reason. The King pressed his case. He must be given access to all areas "if you wish to retain our generous donations and our full support."

But money was not at the bottom of it. The bottom line was the principle that the King should be allowed to enter all parts of his kingdom. Clearly it was Theoderic's intention to wrong-foot Columbanus and produce a copy of his letter to the Pope as evidence of the Irishman's refusal to accept the King's writ.

Columbanus must have known he had been outwitted and cursed his own cleverness. He fell back on that old armoury of teachers through the ages. He threatened Theoderic that if he pursued his persecution of the monastery he would bring about the "destruction of his kingdom and the scattering of all his race" (*ibid.*).

Well that's what Jonas says he said, but probably he never said anything of the sort because the King seized his opportunity and told him that any of the monastic community who wished to cut themselves off completely from all men must leave Burgundy and return to the place from which they had come. Columbanus declared that he would not leave Luxeuil unless dragged by force. It was sheer bravado on his part but the King wisely realised that to be seen dragging an elderly and much respected man from his home would not play well on whatever was the seventh century equivalent of the evening news. He remounted his horse and rode away.

He must have known that for Columbanus forcible repatriation would mean certain death (another good reason for suggesting that he did not leave Ireland entirely of his own volition). Columbanus appears to have known it also. However he didn't have any choice. Theoderic's lieutenant, a minor landowner named Count Baudulf, carted Columbanus and his few remaining Irish brethren off "into exile" to Besancon. Only the Irish monks were forced to leave. The rest of the monks at the three monasteries were Franks or Gauls and they were allowed to stay.

Still there weren't many of the Irishmen left, only five that we know of, plus Columbanus makes a party of six. One of them, Diecola, the brother of Gall, didn't get very far, possibly not even as far as Besancon. He fell ill and being very elderly — all the Irishmen were in their late sixties by now — he was allowed to create a hermitage for himself and stay behind (O'Fiaich, 1990, p. 35). Possibly this was a ruse as he recovered well enough to found his own monastery at Lure, only a few miles from Luxeuil and is remembered in the name of the French town of St Die.

However the hostility the Irishmen faced from the local bishops and aristocracy is illustrated in a story told of Diecola's attempts to set up a hermitage. A local chaplain (and therefore an employee of the local bishop) who was unhappy at having a hermit in his congregation barricaded the chapel with thorn bushes to keep him out and the nobleman who owned the chapel had Diecola beaten. Having regard to the circumstances of their departure from Luxeuil it is unlikely this aggressive response was simply the result of professional jealousy. The nobleman duly fell sick and Diecola was summoned to help him. After the man was healed through his prayers his wife gave Diecola the chapel and land around it but we should note he eventually built the abbey of Lure on land given to him by King Lothar II (Matz, 2000, p. 21).

At Besancon it appears they were initially thrown into prison as Jonas tells us Columbanus asked for permission to preach to the convicts. The tale has overtones of stories from the Acts of Apostles — the freeing of Peter from prison for example and his fetters bursting asunder, or Paul and Silas converting their jailer — but reading between the lines it seems the monks escaped and sought sanctuary in the church at Besancon (Jonas, pp. 18–19). At first they were locked out with the King's men bearing down on them but one of the monks climbed over the wall and was able to let them in just in the nick of time.

The local bishop, Nicetius, was either unusually friendly or more probably put in an impossible position. After Gregory of Tours had made such a song and dance about standing firm on the principle of sanctuary he could hardly hand over his fellow-churchmen. He was honour bound to offer them his protection.

The King sent troops to fetch the monks out of the church. Columbanus at first resolutely (and sensibly) refused to budge. The situation became so heated that the King sent his own chamberlain, Count Bertechar, and his captain Ragamund to expel the monks personally.

Jonas invests the event with his usual drama.

"I left my native land for the love of Christ", he has Columbanus say, "I shall not leave this place unless I am forced to."

And he probably did say something of the sort.

Nicetius was between a rock and a hard place. Somehow he managed to broker a safe conduct and, seeing that he was placing the lives of the bishop and his congregation in danger by remaining obdurate Columbanus surrendered. Captain Ragamund — having given them his personal assurance of their safety — escorted the dwindling band of Irishmen — Lua, Eunoc, Gall and Domoal together with Columbanus at their head — all the way across Gaul to Nantes. They passed through Autun, Saulieu and Avallon where Columban saw off an assassination attempt which Jonas represents as an attack by a horseman suffering from demonic possession which Columbanus miraculously cured. Five more demons were vanquished near Vezelay and the twelve in the residence of Theodemanda outside Auxerre already mentioned.

At Auxerre itself which Lothar II had just lost to Theoderic, Columbanus further got up the nose of his persecutors by prophesying that despite this setback within three years Lothar would be King of Burgundy. This presience was given to him with hindsight but he may well have made an accurate prediction that Theoderic was on a collision course with the other kings and headed for a fight which ultimately he would not win.

After Nevers the journey got easier as they were able to travel by water along the Loire. When one of the soldiers tried to hurry the elderly Lua by striking him with an oar Columbanus intervened threatening him with divine vengeance for his disrespect. With some satisfaction Jonas reports the man drowned on the return journey.

From Nevers they sailed to Orleans where all the churches were closed against them (in case they should again seek sanctuary) and they found it difficult to obtain food. A "Syrian" woman and her husband came to their rescue reminding us of the close alliance between the Celtic Church and the refugee Copts.

At Tours they were refused permission to land. The tomb of St Martin in the cathedral was a famous sanctuary and the King was clearly taking no chances. Nevertheless Jonas tells us Columbanus spent the night in prayer at the tomb of St Martin. Since he was not allowed to land in Tours this was probably at the church in the village of Candes in the same diocese where St Martin actually died. His remains were "translated" to Tours rather inelegantly by passing them out of a window to avoid the monks from Poitiers pinching them. The poor man had hardly been laid out at the time.

Candes had also in recent years seen a hot dispute between the then Bishop of Tours, Gregory, and a man named Pelagius. Gregory finds all sorts of reasons for this dispute but the man's name might be a bit of a clue. That Columbanus should choose this spot to pay his respects to St Martin rather than the cathedral at Tours was in itself a silent expression of his opinion.

Perhaps for this reason he was invited to dine with the current Bishop of Tours, Leoparius, although not presumably in the city. He probably had a country estate nearby. The dinner was not a success. Columbanus got into a row with a relative of Theoderic's and ended by repeating his prophecy that the king would lose his crown within three years. His mood is illustrated by the fact that he uncharitably refers to "that dog Theoderic" (Jonas, p. 23).

Eventually they reached Nantes at the mouth of the Loire and here Captain Ragamund, having fulfilled his oath of safe conduct, left them. They were placed in the custody of the local Bishop, Sofronius, who kept them, if not in prison, at least under house arrest until their ship could sail but then their guards were curiously withdrawn.

Columba wrote to Attala, his replacement as Abbot at Luxeuil:

> ... as I write a messenger has arrived with the news that the ship is ready for me. By it I'll be carried unwillingly to my homeland. If I flee, however, there's no guard to prevent it, for they seem to want me to escape (O'Fiaich, 1990, p. 79).

Columbanus was no fool. He was in an impossible position. If he boarded the ship and allowed himself to be returned to Ireland he would be killed. If he made a run for it he would be cut down. He seems to have toyed with the idea of suggesting the Irish solution of being set adrift in a boat without sail or oars and allowing God or the current to decide the matter (Jonas, p. 24). If the proposal was ever put it must have been rejected because he and his fellow monks were put on board a ship bound for Ireland and set sail.

There was nothing left for them to do but pray.

So they prayed.

And their prayers were answered.

A great storm blew up and the ship ran aground on a sandbar. For the proper biblical three days the captain struggled to refloat it. Eventually, superstitious like all seamen, he declined to take the Irishmen any further and set them ashore. Miraculously the ship began to float and sailed off into the blue.

The Irish monks once again had their feet on dry land but whose dry land? To return to Nantes meant certain death. The land on which they were set ashore was probably Belle Isle just north of the mouth of the Loire and it would have been a short boat ride from there to the coast of Brittany. In Brittany they would have found other sympathetic Celts to assist them.

Was it at this moment, when his prayers were so clearly and unequivocally answered, that Columbanus made up his mind that he would not abandon the struggle. In his advice to a young disciple he says "Though weary don't give up".

Was it at this moment that he made up his mind that he would retrace his steps and go even further, he would take the fight all the way to Rome.

Chapter 14

The Constant Sea

The fugitives were able to travel across Brittany avoiding the territory of Theoderic, where their lives would have been forfeit, until they reached the lands controlled by Lothar II, the second of Columbanus' adopted sons.

They stayed for some time with Lothar who seems to have been quite devoted to Columbanus. Jonas tells us "He now received Columban as a veritable gift from heaven and begged that he would remain in Neustria" (Jonas, p. 25).

Columbanus was happy to stay for a time but declined to make a permanent home with him as he did not wish to add to his problems or encourage enmity between him and the other kings.

In any case events intervened.

While he was at Lothar's court war broke out between Theodebert and Theoderic—yet another of the interminable boundary disputes that contributed to the fratricidal tendencies of the Merovingians. Embassies arrived from both brothers to seek the support of Lothar who was, according to Jonas, disposed to aid one against the other but asked Columban's advice in the matter. Columban "filled with the spirit of prophecy, advised Lothar not to ally himself to either for within three years he would acquire both kingdoms" (*ibid.*).

The spirit of prophecy notwithstanding this was sound advice and illustrates the position of trust and respect Columban held at the Frankish courts. However, Columbanus was himself it seems disposed to go to the aid of Theodebert. His old friend the Queen Mother is not mentioned by Jonas at this point so it seems likely that she had died by this time. Lothar provided him with an armed escort for his protection — another indication of the importance he attached to Columban's role as an advisor and diplomat — and his party set off for Paris — indicating that they had met up with Lothar probably at Chartres or Le Mans, just across the border from Brittany.

Theodebert unfortunately for them was on the other side of the country at Metz so their journey took them via Paris, outside which Columbanus cast out another devil, perhaps indicating they evaded assassination or capture again there when they were not too far north of Theodemanda's estates at Auxerre for her to still be able to strike at them.

At Meaux in the valley of the Marne they found refuge with a former benefactor whose name was Chagneric. One of his sons, whose name was Chagnoald, was a monk at Luxeuil. Here Columbanus blessed his nine-year old daughter Fara, the future abbess of the famous monastery of Faremoutiers where Bede tells us the Anglo-Saxon Kings of England chose to have their children educated. Further along the Marne they stayed with another landowner and his wife who asked the Abbot to bless their children.

By means of these artless stories of children touched by the hand of the saint Jonas demonstrates for us the depth of influence that Columbanus had throughout Gaul. Of the children blessed on that occasion one son, Ado, became the founder of the double monastery of Joane, another, Audoan, was the founder of Rebais. A third brother, Rado, was the chief benefactor of the monastery of Reuil.

When Columbanus reached the court of Theodebert Jonas tells us he was received with "great joy".

"Many of his brothers", Jonas reports, "had already come to the court from Luxeuil and he greeted them as if they had been snatched from the hands of the enemy" (*ibid.*, p. 26). This was probably not far from the truth because we learn a little later that Theoderic and his mistress "were venting their wrath not only on Columban but also on the holy Desiderius, Bishop of Vienne" (*ibid.*, p. 27). Clearly they had been having something of a purge of recalcitrant churchmen because among the refugee monks at Metz, Columban

finds Eustasius and Attala, who had replaced him as tempo-
rary Abbot.

In what is perhaps a postscript to the letter he wrote at
Nantes before being forced to set sail for Ireland
Columbanus appears to suggest that he and his party are
now safely arrived in Brittany. This last section of the letter
reads as if it has been added as the paragraph before refers
to the arrival of the messenger with news that the ship is
ready and seems to be the end of the original letter.

> Moreover [he writes], if you see perfection further
> removed from you than before, and fate keeps me away
> from you, and Attala is not strong enough to govern you,
> then as your brethren [i.e. the monks who had accompa-
> nied him to Nantes?] are here in the neighbourhood of the
> Bretons, unite yourselves altogether in one group... Mean-
> while let the man whom you have all elected be over you
> because if I'm free to do so, I'll take care of you God willing
> (O'Fiaich, 1990, pp. 79–80).

It sounds as if he has already heard something of Attala's
difficulties and is, in cautious terms, letting his friends at
Luxeuil know his intention to start again on his own terms.

Chagneric's son Chagnoald also joined him at Theodebert's
court and was no doubt pleased to hear news of his family.
Bobelin and Ursicinius are other names we know and a few
others had also made the journey to Metz so that
Columbanus again had with him the requisite twelve companions to help him found another monastery.

However they still had to face the opposition of the
French bishops, as well as the hostility of Theoderic and his
mistress, and Columbanus still had it in mind to take his
case personally to the Pope at some stage. Theodebert, we
are told, "promised to seek out beautiful places suitable for
God's servants" (Jonas, p. 26) and true to his word offered
them a choice of possible refuges. With all these things in
mind Columban, with the approval of his companions, settled on a place called Tuggen, on the south-east shore of
Lake Constance.

This area was peopled with fellow Celts which would
have made settlement easier for them and there was a
Christian community on the south side of the lake at Arbon

Boat builders at Richmond
This is the type of boat that Columbanus
would have used to row up the Rhine

Early 7th-century ornaments from Lombardy
typical of the Court of Agilulf and Theodelinda
(Housed in British Museum)

where they would find friends. However the object of their mission was to carry the Gospel to the pagan Allemani, the German tribes on the north side of the lake who still worshipped Woden and the other Teutonic deities.

The easiest way to accomplish this long journey from Metz in the north was by water so they first sailed north down the Moselle to the confluence with the Rhine at Koblenz, then turned south into the great waterway that would take them all the way up to Switzerland. The spectacular Rhine gorge requires good oarsmen and sailors. The legend of the Lorelei rock, a steep and dramatic cliff where a siren was said to sing and lure boatmen to their doom, grew out of the dangerous currents and volatile weather conditions which could easily drive a wooden vessel onto the rocks and smash it to pieces.

To hearten his crew Columbanus composed his most famous surviving poem, a boating song in which we get a flavour of the difficulties of the journey — and a reference to the dangerous situation from which they had already escaped.

Columban's Boating Song

Lo little bark on the twin-horned Rhine
From forests hewn to skim the brine
Heave, lads, and let the echoes ring.

The tempests howl, the storms dismay,
But manly strength can win the day
Heave, lads, and let the echoes ring.

For clouds and squalls will soon pass on
And victory lie with work well done
Heave, lads, and let the echoes ring.

Hold fast! survive! And all is well,
God sent you worse, he'll calm this swell,
Heave, lads, and let the echoes ring.

So Satan acts to tire the brain
And by temptation, souls are slain,
Think, lads, of Christ and echo him.

Stand firm in mind 'gainst Satan's guile,
Protect yourselves with virtue's foil,
Think, lads, of Christ and echo him.

Strong faith and zeal will victory gain,
The old foe breaks his lance in vain,
Think, lads, of Christ and echo him.

The King of virtues vowed a prize
For him who wins, for him who tries
Think, lads, of Christ and echo him .

(O'Fiaich, 1990, pp. 42–4)

At Basel Ursicinius left them to carry the word of the Gospel into the mountains of the Jura (from where he could more easily keep in contact with their base camp at Luxeuil). Here he created for himself a hermitage which provided the basis of the future Abbey of St Ursanne.

Following the Rhine tributaries the rest of the party arrived at Tuggen. Here they settled themselves and began their mission of carrying Christianity to the pagan Allemani.

This does not seem to have been a success.

Columbanus, as we have seen, had a 'softly, softly' approach to evangelism. It was an axiom of his methods that conversion should take place by means of reasonable persuasion and gradual assimilation. Toleration was after all at the heart of his plea to allow the Celtic church a place at the heart of Europe.

He must have been quite appalled when Gall, one supposes in an excess of missionary zeal, set fire to the pagan temple and threw the offerings and idols of the Allemani into the lake (*ibid.*, pp. 43–4).

The pagans, not surprisingly, reacted angrily. Columbanus learned of a plot to murder Gall and prudently withdrew his forces, although not quickly enough to save himself. Gall, being taller and somewhat younger, managed to leg it but Columbanus was caught and severely beaten although the tribesmen stopped short of doing the old man serious injury. It's not surprising that after this, relations were soured between the two men (Lehane, 2005, p. 173).

They retreated to Arbon on the southern shore where the Christian community sheltered them. The priest was a man named Willimar and three of his deacons later joined Gall in setting up his monastic foundation at the town which bears his name. Here they learned of an abandoned Roman fort some fifteen miles away at the end of the lake called Brigantium (modern Bregenz). Three times they had successfully utilised an old Roman fort to set up their foundations so, keeping to the pattern which had worked so well at Anagrates, Luxeuil and Fontaine, they set off for Bregenz.

As well as all the mod cons a Roman fort provided Brigantium also had a Christian church, a ruined chapel now which had originally been dedicated to St Aurelia then converted to a pagan temple. The new residents re-consecrated it to Christian worship. In his life of St Gall, Walafrid Strabo explains how they did it.

First Gall preached to the pagans calling on them to turn away from the worship of brazen images which he took down from the walls, broke up and threw again into the lake. Some who revered the old gods took umbrage and departed in a rage but they were presumably fewer in number in this locality and no violence ensued. Enough remained to hear what these new Christians had to offer.

Columbanus blessed water and sprinkled it around the building while the monks walked in procession around it chanting psalms. The Abbot anointed the altar with oil and having placed the relics of St Aurelia within it (presumably they were found to be buried in the chapel) he put a new altar cloth over it and celebrated Mass.

The attractions of Bregenz seem to have induced a mixed response among its new residents. According to the Life of St Gall the monks, and Gall almost certainly, loved it there but Jonas reports — presumably informed by monks who went with Columbanus to Italy — that he didn't like it. Gall and his companions spoke the local language which perhaps explains why they felt more at home.

The new monastery was set up sometime towards the end of 610 AD and the first year of the foundation seems to have passed peacefully enough. Perhaps on the shores of the lovely Lake Constance the wistful hope of a stable life began to creep into their minds but it was not to be. While they were quietly building their cloisters, clearing their fields and planting fruit trees, events in the outside world had again changed the balance of power.

Columban was so alarmed at the prospect of impending disaster for Theodebert that Jonas tells us he travelled to see the king and advised him to abdicate voluntarily and enter a monastery – not as it turned out as secure a prospect as the elderly Abbot evidently imagined. In any case Theodebert laughed off the suggestion saying Merovingian kings did not give up their kingdoms so easily.

Once again Columban's political judgement was to prove unerring. His acute understanding of the weakness of Theodebert's military position adds weight to the probability that it was he, and not Columcille, who was forced to leave Ireland following a military victory that left the opposing army all but massacred.

The war between Theoderic and Theodebert ended in a victory for Theoderic, first at Toul and then at the battle of Tolbiac where their great-great-grandfather Clovis had first founded the Frankish kingdom. It is now the German town of Zulpich between Aachen and Bonn. The battle resulted in great slaughter and Theodebert was taken into captivity by Count Bertechar, Theoderic's chamberlain. It is possible that it was at this point, rather than before the battle, that Columban attempted to intervene and try and negotiate a settlement between the brothers that would at least leave Theodebert with his life.

The suggestion that Theodebert might abdicate voluntarily and enter a monastery may have raised eyebrows among the Frankish nobility but it was a perfectly sensible one. It was frequently used in the Eastern Empire (along with blinding) as a way of eliminating rivals without the necessity of putting them to death and creating a potential martyr. Once tonsured the rival would be incarcerated in a monastery effectively under house arrest. He would never be allowed to leave the confines of the monastery so was in effect facing a life sentence.

Theoderic we are told was a passive and docile young man and inclined to do as he was told. Like many a passive and docile young man he was clearly putty in the hands of a strong woman but he still had great respect for Columbanus and on this occasion filial respect and family affection won the day. Whatever his feelings in the matter before the battle when he turned down the offer, after he had suffered a crushing defeat Theodebert really had no choice. He was allowed to enter a monastery.

If Columbanus was successful in his negotiations, or believed himself to be, his relief was short-lived. Theoderic's mistress had other ideas. A few days after Theodebert was allowed to enter the monastery, Jonas tells us, she "mercilessly had him murdered". She had good reason. While Theodebert lived, even though he had formally abdicated, he was still potentially an heir to Theoderic's kingdom, as long as her sons remained — as it seems they did — regarded as illegitimate. However, in murdering her lover's kinsman, Theodemanda evoked a blood-feud with Lothar which she would later come to regret.

For the present her star appeared to be in the ascendant. She had eliminated one of the potential legal heirs to Theoderic's throne and now she produced another card from up her sleeve. The Three Chapters Controversy now once again became an issue.

The Code of Justinian proposed three items which were a continuing cause of contention in European politics.

Firstly, it acknowledged the ecclesiastical leadership of the Roman Catholic Church and ordered all Christian groups to submit to her authority. The Celts and Arians took exception to this. While the Celtic Church had no objection to nominally accepting the leadership of the Pope they had strong objections to being ordered to do anything at all.

Secondly, it proclaimed the dominion of the Emperor over the Church. All ecclesiastical, like all civil law, was to emanate from the throne. The whole history of the early middle ages in Europe is one of a constant battle between Church and State as to which should have supreme authority, the ecclesiastical or secular powers. If the Church was held to hold authority over the secular arm in Western Europe, in practice this would have meant all the sovereign states of the West returning to the position of being subject states of the Empire.

But for our purposes here the most significant alteration was the third item on the agenda. The ancient privilege of agnate[1] relatives, that is relatives in the male line, inheriting intestate property (that is property where there is no named legitimate heir) was now to switch to the cognate[2] relatives in direct line, that is the children and grandchildren of the dead person. Thus, under Salic law, which operates according to the agnatic principle, Edward III could not inherit the throne of France legally since his claim was traced through his mother.

The normal practice among the Frankish kings had been for kingdoms to be divided between the surviving agnate relatives. This principle had also operated in early Roman law. However the Codex of the Emperor Justinian in the early sixth century had introduced some important changes especially in relation to the position of women. As Will Durant explains in *The Age of Faith*:

> The status of woman was moderately improved by the Code. Her subjection to lifelong guardianship had been ended in the fourth century and the old principle that inheritance could pass only through males had become obsolete (Durant, 1950, p. 113).

It seems that the French bishops (and behind them the Eastern Empire) at last saw a way to re-establish their authority over Gaul through their support of Theoderic and his consort—especially the latter, who clearly had a big stake in the switch from the Salic to the Justinian legal code.

---

[1] Agnate, agnation: In Roman law *agnati* were kinsfolk, men and women, related to each other by descent from a common male ancestor and who were under a single authority in the family. In modern usage the term is restricted to men only, without reference to a common familial authority, so that an agnate is one related by descent through males only. Commonly the preferred term is patrilineal (Mitchell, 1964, p. 4).

[2] Cognate, cognatic—two persons are cognates when they are able to trace their descent from a common ancestor or ancestress regardless of whether the links are through males or females. Thus a cognatic kinship syste is bilateral, observing no unilineal principle (*ibid.*, p. 31).

When commentators suggest that Columbanus did not understand the Three Chapters Controversy, that now re-occupied the Pope's attention, I think they are quite wrong. Not only did he understand it but he understood only too well the political implications for the whole of Gaul if Theodemanda got her way.

The way this controversy now comes to the fore gives weight to the theory that Theoderic's relationship with his mistress was somehow incestuous, and that was the reason not only Columbanus but the entire Frankish Royal Family were horrified by the partnership. Possibly she was his half-sister. We know that Childebert had more than one wife and several mistresses.

She had tried to assert her right to the throne through her marriage but when this failed it appears that she found in the Justinian Code the opportunity to stake her claim and that of her son as a descendent of Childebert. Under Salic law her sons could only inherit if they were publicly acknowledged as Theoderic's legitimate heirs. Under the Code of Justinian she could claim to be Queen of Austrasia in her own right.

Theoderic and Theodemanda between them now controlled Austrasia and Burgundy. With the death of Theodebert and the promotion of the Three Chapters Controversy the Queen's tactics became quite clear.

Columbanus can only have been marginally surprised when the order came for him and his monks to leave Bregenz which now came under her jurisdiction. A trumped-up charge of interfering with local hunting laws was levelled at them by the Duke Gunzo and to show he meant business two of the monks were found murdered in the forest when they went to recover straying cattle. Columbanus was a brave man but he was not foolhardy. The time had come for them to move on.

He returned to his original plan of taking his case personally to the papal court in Rome. Not all the monks were keen to go. Eustasius and Chagnoald returned to Luxeuil. As from their names they were respectively Gallo-Roman and Frankish, the deportation order placed on the Irishmen did not apply and Columbanus perhaps wished to have some men he could trust at the mother-house who could keep him informed as to what was going on at the court in Metz.

Gall, we have already noted, was comfortable on the shore of the lake. He liked fishing and spoke the local language fluently. He felt settled at last. Despite his initial run-in with the pagan Allemani he decided to stay. He claimed to have fallen sick of a fever and to be too ill to travel the long distance over the Alps to Italy. Columbanus, who perhaps knew a psychosomatic illness when he saw one, didn't believe him. Maybe he thought that Gall too intended to slope off back to Luxeuil when his back was turned or thought he was merely being selfish when so much that was important to the Celtic Church was at stake.[3]

At all events they quarrelled violently. Gall refused to go and Columbanus left in a huff forbidding him ever to celebrate Mass again while he (Columbanus) lived (O'Fiaich, 1990, pp. 47–8). This seems a bit harsh but as he was nearly seventy and was about to embark on a trip across the highest mountains in Europe it was not perhaps as stringent a sentence as it sounds.

Columbanus was clearly disappointed in Gall. They had come so far together all the way from Bangor and shared many adventures. He had assumed they would share this last one but for Gall it was a step too far. He remained behind but he was as good as his word and did not return to Luxeuil. He founded the monastery in the town that bears

---

[3]   There is another possible explanation for the row between Columban and Gall. The Life of St Gall mentions that "Gall delivered from the demon by which she was possessed Fridiburga, the daughter of Cunzo and the betrothed of Sigibert, King of the Franks; the latter through gratitude granted to the saint an estate near Arbon which belonged to the royal treasury that he might found a monastery there". This Sigibert would be the illegitimate son of Theoderic and Theodemanda. Sigibert did not become King of the Franks (or rather make that claim) until after Theoderic's death but this close connection with his betrothed might have already rung alarm bells with Columbanus. It is possible that Columbanus accused Gall of selling out to the opposition. See *Catholic Encyclopedia* http://www.newadvent.org/callen/06346b.htm.

his name (St Gallen) which became one of the most influential centres of scholarship in Europe.

But Columbanus was right. Since the defeat of Theodebert Theoderic had control of two-thirds of Francia and the Roman bishops could push the Celtic Church back to the North-west and Brittany. They could and almost certainly would undo all the work that Columbanus had done over the past eighteen years.

Accompanied by two companions, Attala, who was to succeed him at Bobbio as he had done at Luxeuil, and Sigibert, he set off into the harsh conditions of the Alpine region. At the foot of the St Gothard pass at Chur they lost Sigibert who settled into a hermitage which later provided the foundations for the monastery of Disentis.

Columbanus and Attala continued over the pass 7,500 feet above sea-level and finally began their descent into the Ticino valley down to Locarno at the head of Lake Maggiore. From the heights they could see the plain of Lombardy stretching out ahead of them. From winter they moved into summer as they made their way down to the lake. It must have seemed like entering Paradise.

But the worm was already in the apple.

From Brigantium [Bregenz] to Bobbio

Chapter 15

A New Start

As Columbanus and Attala made their way down the valley of the Maggia River towards Lake Maggiore it must have seemed heaven after the rigorous climb through the snowy wastes of the high alpine pass. Stretched before them lay the plain of Lombardy with its beautiful lakes and mild climate. For two quite elderly men the warmth and beauty of the region must have induced in them feelings of bliss. However it was not long before the world they had left behind began to intrude again.

They had hardly crossed the frontier when Columbanus received a letter from the Bishop of Como, whose name was Aggripinus, warning him that the Pope, Boniface IV, formerly treasurer to Gregory the Great, was suspected of being a Nestorian. This was a pretty grave accusation as the Nestorians were anathametized in the "Three Chapters" in the code of Justinian as heretics.

Why should the Bishop of Como wish to suggest the Pope was a heretic and why in particular a Nestorian? Very little is known about Pope Boniface IV but no-one else seems to have specifically accused him of heresy apart from Columbanus himself. Of the very little we do know about Pope Boniface the one thing we can be sure of is that he was stout in his defence of the Three Chapters. (See further the *Additional Note* at the end of this chapter, p. 189.)

If Aggripinus's purpose was to draw from Columbanus some expression of support for Boniface, that could be construed as heresy, thus giving the bishops of Lombardy a stick to beat him with, he mistook his man. Columbanus had not survived twenty-eight years of tortuous Frankish diplomacy without learning a trick or two.

As soon as he reached Milan, Columbanus shot off two letters. One, which unfortunately is not extant, was to the slippery Aggripinus, presumably thanking him for his hospitality and smartly pointing out his error. The gist of his letter was evidently that he, Columbanus, did not believe a word of these scurrilous rumours and he was utterly loyal to the Pope and to his Trinitarian principles.

The second, addressed to Pope Boniface IV, is rather more intriguing. If the Bishop of Como's allegations were genuine — and the Pope was unpopular with the Roman bishops of Lombardy — he might need allies in the Celtic Church. The tone of Columbanus' letter is unusually unctuous but he was in a tricky position and in serious need of allies himself.

His message is subtly conveyed in images, vague allusions to some sort of conspiracy against which he, as a friend, is offering to warn the Pope.

> I'll speak as a friend, a disciple and one who follows in your footsteps, not as a stranger. Therefore I'll speak out freely and say to those who are our pilots and captains and mystical watches of the spiritual ship; Look out! for the sea is stormy and is being lashed by fatal gusts... It is a tempest of the entire element, surging up everywhere and convulsed on every side, that threatens the mystical vessel with shipwreck. Hence I, a frightened sailor, dare scream: Look out! for the water has already entered the vessel of the Church and the ship is in peril (O'Fiaich, 1990, pp. 80–1).

It is tempting to see in his imagery something of the terrifying experience of shipwreck he had suffered at Nantes. Otherwise, unless he seriously believed the Bishop of Como was plotting a coup, it is sheer guff. He goes on to the meat of the matter to emphasise the orthodoxy of the Celtic Church (thus pulling the rug from under the Bishop of Como) and to defend his own record against those who accused him of heresy.

> For all we Irish, inhabitants of the world's edge, are disciples of Saints Peter and Paul and of all the disciples who wrote the sacred canon by the Holy Spirit. We accept noth-

ing outside the evangelical and apostolic teaching. None of us was a heretic, no-one a Jew, no-one a schismatic, but the Catholic faith as it was first transmitted by you (the Popes) successors of the holy apostles, is maintained unbroken (*ibid.*).

He continues by describing how vehement he has been in defending Pope Boniface from allegations of heresy arguing that it was traditional in Ireland to allow a degree of latitude and freedom of speech so that cases might be judged on the basis of the rationality of the argument as an excuse for his own forthright speech, then rather perversely he cautions the Pope to beware of expressing himself too freely,

Thus your honour is great in proportion to the dignity of your See, you need to take equally great care not to lose your reputation through some error.

Finally, and perhaps mindful of the fact that he was now moving into territory where the ascendant theology was that of the Arians he concludes with a plea for religious toleration that has echoed down the ages.

I can't understand how a Christian can quarrel with a Christian about the faith. Whatever an orthodox Christian who rightly glorifies the Lord will say the other will answer Amen because he also loves and believes alike. Let you all therefore say and think the one thing so that all sides 'may be one'[1] — all Christians (*ibid.*).

Having fired off this missive he then settled down in Milan to wait for the Pope's reply no doubt hoping for an invitation to the Papal Curia, perhaps a position at the Pope's side, as a faithfully ally and adviser. This certainly seems to have been his aim because he spent several months in Milan enhancing his reputation for orthodoxy by indulging in debates about the nature of the Trinity with the King's Arian first minister, Ulfilas, and delivering a series of sermons on the subject in the cathedral. He also, according to Jonas, wrote a treatise refuting the Arian arguments, which unfortunately is lost.

However it is clear that his intention was to present himself as entirely respectable and a pillar of the Catholic

---

[1]   John 17.21

Church but even as he was establishing his claim to be considered as worthy of a future position as the Pope's right-hand man the political climate was changing and the extent to which he had misjudged the Roman position was only just coming to light.

Additional Note

The "Three Chapters" refers to a decree of Justinian published in 544 which consisted of brief statements of anathema upon Theodore of Mopsuestria and his writings, upon Theoderet of Cyrus and his writings against St Cyril of Alexandria and the Council of Ephesus and upon the letter written by Ibas of Edessa to Maris, Bishop of Hardaschir in Persia. In other words it anathematized the Nestorians.

To the intense annoyance of the western churches all the popes except Vigilius had accepted and defended the Three Chapters in order to curry favour with their superior, the Emperor in Constantinople. Boniface IV appears to have toed the party line. The one thing we can be fairly sure of is that he was *not* a Nestorian. So why did the Bishop of Como suggest he was?

Nestorius was a contemporary of our own Pelagius. He was born, date unknown, at Germanicia in Syria and died at Panopolis in Egypt circa 451 AD. Having trained as a monk he was appointed Patriarch of Constantinople in April 428 AD. To begin with, ironically as his later career turned out, he was zealous in the persecution of heretics with successful campaigns against first the Arians and then the Novations and Quatrodecimans but not, perhaps significantly, the Pelagians. He came under fire for his leniency towards them and defended himself by saying he did not know enough about them and was seeking further information but the fact was they alone escaped the purge.

So possibly Aggripinus is suggesting obliquely to Columbanus that Pope Boniface IV will be prepared, like Nestorius, to be tolerant towards a "Pelagian" like himself. That's one interpretation.

Nestorius fell foul of his fellow bishops when his domestic chaplain, Anastasius, preached a sermon on the subject of the *Theotokos,* the Mother of God, who had for a long time been identified closely with Mary the mother of Jesus, especially in Constantinople where the Blessed Virgin Mary was the symbol and personification of the city. Anastasius apparently offended everyone by declaring: "Let no-one call Mary the Mother of God, for Mary was a human being, and that God should be born of a human being is impossible."[2]

This, it seems was not entirely Nestorius' view. It seems that he merely wished to separate the identification of Mary as the mother of Jesus from the idea we met earlier when examining what is meant by the Trinity, that the *Theotokos* is properly speaking Sophia or Wisdom or the Holy Spirit. However the popular identification of the Mother City, Constantinople, with the Mother of Jesus, the Blessed Virgin Mary led to what had perhaps been intended as an intellectual discussion of the precise meaning of *Theotokos* creating a major scandal.

Nestorius was in any case unpopular with his fellow bishops who thought him arrogant and one in particular, Cyril of Alexandria, was determined to bring him down. He was condemned as a heretic by the Council of Ephesus in 431 AD and from there it was all downhill. After many tribulations he ended up an exile in the Egyptian desert at Panopolis where he died in 451 AD.

Neither Columbanus nor Pope Boniface IV appear to have been involved in any controversy regarding the cult of Mariolatry. One of the few facts we do know about Boniface IV is that he converted the Roman temple of the Pantheon in Rome into a Christian Church (with a large donation from the Emperor in Constantinople) and dedicated it to "Our Lady and all the Martyrs" so it seems unlikely that it is this aspect of Nestorianism that the Bishop of Como has in mind.

---

[2]   www.1911encyclopedia.org/Nestorius

It was when he was exiled in the desert that Nestorius wrote a book called "The Bazaar of Heracleides of Damascus". It was mentioned by Ebedjesu, a fourteenth century Syrian metropolitan but afterwards it seemed to have been lost until it was discovered relatively recently and translated from Syriac into French in 1910.

It is now thought that the title is a mistranslation and that the title should properly be simply "The Book or Treatise of Heracleides of Damascus". But who is Heracleides of Damascus? He doesn't appear to exist.

One theory is that 'Heracleides of Damascus' is a pseudonym for Nestorius who wished to protect his book from being destroyed but Friedrich Loofs notes:

> The Syriac translator... had already found the title *Treatise of Heracleides* in his Greek original. He does not seem to have known anything about the meaning of this title. The book itself in its present incomplete condition – about one sixth of the whole is missing – nowhere explains the title. Heracleides is not mentioned at all...And Nestorius has made no effort to conceal his authorship.[3]

He concludes that the book has nothing to do with Heracleides of Damascus but he notes that the missing passages are not in one place but spread throughout the book which suggests strongly that certain passages, for one reason or another, have been removed.

The "of Damascus" may not refer after all to the writer but to the location of the book. Nestorius was writing a commentary on a volume of Heracleides which was to be found in Damascus. If so, it would appear that his commentary or extracts from the original have been removed leaving only his own defence against the allegations of heresy.

In this connection the date of the Syriac translation is worth noting as it is thought to have been translated between 525 AD and 533 AD[4], that is, at about the same time as the Church in Rome was adopting the calculations of the

[3] Full text 'Nestorius and his place in the history of Christian doctrine' by Friedrich Loofs www.archive.org/stream/.../nestoriushisplace 00loofrich_dvju.txt- and English translation by Driver and Hodgson.
[4] It was translated into English by G R Driver and Leonard Hodgson (Oxford, 1925).

Alexandrian mathematicians. Since it was common at the time for classical works to be embedded in later theological ones could this be how the Irish monks came to possess the work of Heracleides? Their Syrian contacts and Nestorius' sympathy with the Pelagians might explain how this work came into their hands.

Since there is no reason to suppose that Pope Boniface IV was a Nestorian we have to ask why the Bishop of Como raises this spectre and why he thinks Columbanus might also have Nestorian sympathies. Did he quote from "The Book of Heracleides" in his work on the dating of Easter? It does deal at length with the doctrine of creation and that section might have been preceded by an extract from Heracleides dealing with the movement of the planets. However, as both this extract — if it existed at all — and Columban's work on the dating of Easter are lost, this has to remain in the realm of pure speculation.

Nevertheless the inference we can draw from the Bishop of Como's letter is that he had reason to suspect Columban of being in some way a Nestorian and therefore a heretic.

Chapter 16

The Road to Rome

Before faith came we were kept under the law, shut away
from the faith which would afterwards be revealed to us.
The law was like our schoolmaster, we were subjected to its
discipline until we might reach an understanding of the
true nature of Christ.

Now that faith has come we are no longer like children
under a schoolmaster but able to govern ourselves. Now
you are all able to become children of God by following the
example of Christ Jesus.

As many of you as have been baptised unto Christ are
capable of becoming Christ.

There is no longer Jew or Greek, there is no longer slave
or free, there is no longer male or female, for all of you are
one in Christ Jesus (Galatians 3.23–8).

This is Paul to the Galatians and when we come to think
how strictly the Roman Empire was stratified at the time of
writing it, it comes home how very revolutionary, not to say
incendiary, this thinking was.

When Paul writes he is thinking primarily (one assumes)
of John's definition of God as an androgynous whole — in
the spiritual plane there is no racial, sexual or class division — such things make no sense in that context. But the
political implications of such a theory in the context of the
Roman Empire where the economy depended on slave
labour, women were regarded as chattels and there was a
clear racial distinction between those who were citizens of
the Empire and the "barbarians" who were subject to it or
outside it were potentially explosive.

By the time Columbanus is writing to the Pope the
Empire has on the face of it disappeared. We have seen that
in the North, particularly those areas that were outside the
Empire — the Frankish and Irish kingdoms in particular —

women were treated, if not as equals, at least as having substantial rights and there was a tradition of free-thinking and
free-speaking.

The social and cultural Empire however persisted to
some extent in southern Britain and throughout Gaul. The
further south you went the stronger the remnants of imperial civilisation held out. The nearer Columbanus came to
Rome the more heretical his ideas would have seemed.

Pelagius — the first heretical Briton — expounded the doctrine of free will which, in spite of Columban's protestations
of orthodoxy, continued to pervade the Celtic Church and
the Northern European mind.

> Within our minds [Pelagius wrote], there is a kind of natu-
> ral sanctity, which we call conscience. This conscience pre-
> sides over the mind as a judge presides over a court. It
> favours honourable and righteous actions and it condemns
> hurtful and wrong actions. Just as a judge is guided by a
> book of law, so the conscience is guided by an inner law
> which has been written on the soul of God. But in one
> important respect the way in which conscience works is
> different from the way a court works. In a court lawyers on
> opposing sides try to win their case by brilliant argument.
> They are not trying to reveal the truth but merely to win the
> judge to their side. Conscience by contrast rejects brilliant
> argument and instead wants only the truth of each and
> every situation, and only when it has discerned the truth
> will conscience make its judgement. When we read the
> scriptures and remark that Moses and Abraham were good
> people, we are simply saying that in their conscience was a
> firm and strong judge. When Adam and Eve ate from the
> tree of knowledge they were exercising their freedom of
> choice, and as a consequence of the choice they made they
> were no longer able to live in the Garden of Eden. Before
> eating the fruit they did not know the difference between
> good and evil; thus they did not possess the knowledge
> which enables human beings to exercise freedom of choice.
> By eating the fruit they acquired this knowledge and from
> this moment onwards they were free. The story of their
> banishment from Eden is in truth the story of how the
> human race gained its freedom by eating fruit from the tree
> of knowledge. Adam and Eve became mature beings
> responsible to God for their actions (Brown, 2006, p. 53).

Paul in his letter to the Galatians offers another example. In the Old Testament Abraham — the ancestor of every-one — has two sons, one who is the son of a slave, the other born to a free woman. This, says Paul, is an *allegory*. Agar, the bondwoman, represents the people in bondage, people we would say without self-government. The free woman, Sarah, is the ancestress of all those who have self-government, who are sufficiently enlightened, as Pelagius suggests, to take responsibility for their own actions.

We think of the foundations of liberal democracy as being laid in the late 17th and early 18th centuries — the Age of Reason — but just as genetecists can now tell you if you are descended from Saxons or Vikings, these ideas did not come out of the ether but were part of the cultural inheri-tance of every European, particularly in the North where the imperial writ ran less confidently and made less impact on the underlying culture.

These are not the dry and dusty musings of almost forgot-ten ancients but are the principles which shape our every-day existence. Christianity is so fundamental to the European mindset that no matter what creed, if any, a mod-ern European adheres to no-one can afford to be ignorant of its intellectual framework.

When Columban arrived in Milan he brought these ideas with him and some of them he found there already in the form of Arianism — the predominant form of Christian phi-losophy favoured by the ruling elite — the Lombards.

The Lombards were fairly recent arrivals in Northern Italy — Gregory of Tours still refers to them as the Langobards — the "longbeards" — a name which according to Paul the Deacon who wrote their history was a reference to their characteristic long beards — as opposed to the Romans who generally preferred to be clean-shaven. That their brand of monotheistic thinking remained a potent force in Europe for many centuries is evidenced by the fact that as late as the twelfth century Henry, Bishop of Winchester, although a Cardinal and a Papal Legate in his time — was accused by some of his detractors of being a "longbeard". He was trained at the monastery of Cluny which seems to have acquired at that time a reputation for free-thinking and was one of the most influential of the Benedictine monasteries in early mediaeval Europe in the North.

By 573 AD the Lombards had captured Verona, Milan, Florence and Pavia which they made their capital. In 601 AD they captured Padua and in 603 AD Cremona and Mantua (Durant, 1950, p. 1). They posed a clear threat to Ravenna, the Italian capital of the Eastern Empire.

We have already seen how the Byzantine Emperor Maurice was prepared to pay heavily to induce the Burgundians under Childebert to invade Lombardy and drive out the long-beards. Childebert took the money but he clearly had no intention of dislodging potential allies. He made a token foray into Lombard territory then promptly declared a truce and signed a peace treaty. The Emperor was furious. The Romans thereafter had no reason to trust either the Lombards or the Franks. Both had thrown off the yoke of imperial conquest and had no intention of inviting it back again. There was an atmosphere of mutual distrust. The Roman bishops were seen as instruments of the Empire — the Pope was still officially the fifth Patriarch answerable to the Emperor.

When Columbanus arrived in Milan at the start of 613 AD the king of Lombardy was Agilulf. He had become king through his marriage to the former queen Theodelinda. She was the daughter of Duke Garibald. Her mother, Garibald's wife, was the daughter of an earlier Lombard king named Waco (d. 540 AD) whose dynasty according to tradition had ruled for at least seven generations so she had the bluest of blue blood. She "chose" Agilulf when her previous husband Authani died. Agilulf had previously been the Duke of Turin. He reigned with Theodelinda from 590 AD until 616 AD. During his reign the kingdom achieved much greater stability and security (Collins, 1999).

Partly this was due to his policy of religious toleration. Agilulf was an Arian but his wife had converted to Roman Catholicism. When is not clear. Possibly this was in itself a political manoeuvre to ensure both sides were equally represented in the state. At all events it seems to have worked well. Agilulf and his queen patronised both Arian and Roman churches and encouraged a spirit of debate and religious scholarship. It was in this context that they gave permission to Columban to cross their borders and made him welcome at the Milanese court.

In truth the differences between Celt and Arian were fairly slight. Pelagianism was reckoned to be a form of Arianism and we have seen how the spirit of Pelagius hovered over the Celtic Church. The principal difference was in the definition of the nature of Jesus and the importance of the Trinity in the intellectual framework of the Celtic Church which, with the Celtic love of triads, was paramount.

Arius taught that only God the Father was eternal and too pure and infinite to appear on the earth. Therefore God produced Christ the Son out of nothing as the first and greatest creation. The Son is then the one who created the universe. Some Arians even held that the Holy Spirit was the first and greatest creation of the Son. The Council of Nicaea condemned Arianism and stated that the Son was co-substantial (of one and the same substance or being) and co-eternal with the Father, a belief formulated as *homoousios* ("of one substance") against the Arian position of *homoiousios* ("of *like* substance"). An illustration of their difference of opinion may be found in the debate between Agilan and Gregory of Tours (pp. 74–75) in which Agilan tries to prove that the Father and Son are separate 'persons' and that one logically must follow the other.

Columban's view was somewhat ambivalent for although in his sermon on Faith he re-iterates the orthodox position with regard to the Trinity in his letter to Pope Boniface IV he chooses his words very carefully noting that "the *Roman* church (my italics) defends no heretic against the Catholic Faith" and suggests that the Pope might consider defending anything that is "*useful* or orthodox"(my italics again). The astronomical data he has championed might come under the heading of 'useful' if not orthodox and he was, as he admits to the Pope, doing the bidding of an Arian King.

It seems that, from the political standpoint of the Celts and Arians, their similarities were more important than any differences. Both were representative of those peoples of Northern Europe who had been conquered or threatened with conquest by the Roman Empire and — even though this was a couple of centuries after the fall of Rome — still resented it.

Initially however it seems that Columban's first approach was to be conciliatory towards Rome and seek an alliance with the Pope. He was after all still officially a Catholic. His principal strategy seems to have been to try and force a synod at which the Celtic position could be successfully argued and carried. He was clearly confident in his own abilities to put his case to the Papal Curia and win hands down. Not without reason because his intellectual gifts and powers of persuasion had stood him in good stead before and he was utterly convinced of the justice of his cause.

Furthermore his Irish charm had clearly not deserted him for although he was now pushing seventy he had in very short order established an affectionate relationship with the queen Theodelinda and gained the indulgent respect of her husband.

His main adversary at the court (apart from the slippery Bishop of Como of whom we hear nothing further) was the first minister, Ulfilas, named after the Arian scholar who first translated the Bible into Gothic.

He and Columbanus staged public debates where each argued his own case in presumably good-natured and perhaps politically motivated intellectual tussles. Such debates were clearly encouraged by Agilulf and Theodelinda since they publicly established their reputation for toleration and free-thinking. At the same time they allowed these prominent thinkers to attack the Three Chapters Controversy and diminish Theodemanda's claim to the thrones of Austrasia and Burgundy, both of which kingdoms were still in her possession.

These encounters were also helpful to Columban as they established *his* reputation as a defender of orthodox Catholicism and undermined any claims the Bishop of Como might make as to his own tendency to heresy. He was arguing *against* the heretics was he not?

To further shore up his position he spent the first half of the year preaching at the cathedral in Milan — sixteen possible sermons (nineteen altogether but three are regarded as doubtful) survive each of which is a model of orthodoxy and suggest a strong desire on his part to impress the Roman bishops.

While Agilulf was no doubt interested in these intelligent exchanges he saw no reason to upset the politically sound status quo so he declined to convert to the Celtic Church, but he continued to support and encourage Columbanus for reasons which were diplomatic rather than theological.

While Columbanus had been waiting in Milan for an invitation to the Papal court which never came, events elsewhere were again shifting the balance of power. Theoderic survived his murdered brother by no more than a year — as Columbanus had apparently rather niftily predicted. Possibly this prophecy was divinely inspired or maybe he just knew the brothers rather well and could put two and two together. At all events — and this is the main thing for a prophet — he was bang on the money.

In 613 AD just after Columbanus had been forced to abandon his new foundation at Bregenz, which must have given the accuracy of his prophecy added potency, Theoderic died in a fire. The circumstances of the fire are not clear and in an age of wooden buildings fires were not uncommon but from a political point of view it was convenient. His "widow" now had sole control of two-thirds of Gaul.

According to Frankish custom Theoderic's kingdom now devolved to the remaining legitimate agnate male relative, that is to his cousin Lothar II. This meant that Lothar was now heir to all of Gaul, giving Chilperic and Fredegund the last laugh.

For the Roman bishops, not to mention the new Emperor Heraclius, this must have been a horrific prospect. Lothar supported the Celtic Church and was not likely to be amenable to any deal with the Byzantines. The Papacy was being pushed back into the west of Italy (the East being still the province of the Eastern Orthodox Church). The Western Roman Empire, or what was left of it, far from expanding into the heart of Europe, stood to lose even that precarious foothold. It's not surprising therefore that the Pope and the Emperor looked for another candidate to back.

Lothar inherited under Frankish law, but as we have seen in the preceding chapter, Roman law, in the form of the Justinian codex, allowed an intestate estate to be inherited by a female relative with a common ancestor. Under this law, Theodemanda, if she were indeed the daughter of Childebert, could inherit both kingdoms of Austrasia and Burgundy from her half-brother Theoderic giving her control of two-thirds of Gaul. The Emperor Heraclius could then revive the strategy of attacking the Lombard kingdom from the north and east and strike out from Austrasia into Lothar's hands.

The Lombards and Franks were faced with a very dangerous situation and we have already seen how alive Columban was to military strategy. Here we have a clue as to why the supposedly heretical Nestorian Pope Boniface IV suddenly changed direction and began to propound the principles of the Three Chapters[1] and why Columbanus equally vigorously began to oppose it.

It has been suggested that Columban did not understand the dispute over the Three Chapters but I have already indicated that I think he understood the political implications of it very well. We are told that Theodelinda was initially in favour of the Three Chapters as she may well have been since she would have been able to inherit her father's throne under this law instead of being obliged to hand it over to her

[1]   In fact by this date the argument seems to have moved beyond the Three Chapters, which was a purely theological document, to acceptance of the Codex Constitutionem of 529 and Roman law in general.

husband. Columbanus, despite the evidence that he otherwise encouraged equality between men and women, persuaded her to abandon her support. The potential danger to the Lombard state overrode a commitment to female emancipation.[2]

It was Theodemanda who stood to benefit from the switch to Roman law as a model for conducting European affairs since her claim and that of her sons depended on it. Lothar's claim was supported by Salic law, the native law of the Franks. If he would not recognise the legitimacy of her marriage and therefore her sons' inheritance under that law she would achieve the same result by changing the law completely. Her sons could then inherit legally through her rather than their father and in the meantime she could reign as a Queen in her own right. Even the first Brunhild had not been able to do that.

There was also the question of the Pope's standing in the East. With Antioch gone, with Jerusalem under threat and soon to fall, with Damascus in peril, only the patriarchs of Constantinople and Rome were left to give their support to the Empire. Suddenly the patriarch of Rome had an unprecedented influence at the Court of Constantinople. With a rapprochement with the Emperor Pope Boniface could shore up his position in Italy if nothing else.

To the no doubt growing unease of Columbanus and his royal patrons, the Kings of Francia and Lombardy, the Pope's hitherto supposed heretical tendencies now unfolded themselves into a new flowering of the Three Chapters Controversy, the ultimate aim of which was the reunification of the whole of the Roman Empire, ruled from Constantinople using the church to impose uniformity by ideological rather than military means thereby indirectly effecting the re-conquest of the West. The accession of Heraclius who was a soldier of some distinction made the likelihood that he would look for a military solution even more probable.

The weaker the Empire grew along its Eastern borders, the more provincial capitals it lost to the expanding Arab

[2]   Lehane, 2005, p. 176.

empires, the more likely it was that the Emperor would look to expand his territories westwards back into the heartlands of the old Roman imperium.

Theoderic and his consort had, until Theoderic's death, controlled two thirds of Gaul, once Theodebert had been disposed of, and they had, of necessity, needed to rely heavily on the support of the Roman magnates and metro-politans, who were not slow to take the opportunity to shore up imperial interests and influence in the region. Were the Pope to lose control of Austrasia and Burgundy to Lothar this would be very bad news indeed for the future of both Church and Empire. His sphere of influence would be reduced to western Italy alone, excluding the north and south at that, and the barely Roman Catholic parts of Eng-land that were under the sway of the Anglo-Saxon kings who had converted who were still fairly thin on the ground.

The re-run of the Three Chapters Controversy was a timely attempt to shore up the power of Theodemanda and legitimise the claim of her sons who, in the eyes of the Franks at least, seem to have remained illegitimate. Lothar never recognised his cousin's sons as having any rights at all. (Whereas Guntram had recognised his rights and those of Childebert when he stood as uncle/regent for them.) The Merovingians may have been generally lax in their sexual relations but they were very strict when it came to the issue of legitimacy.

In Milan the news of these developments was met with a flurry of diplomatic activity. For Columbanus going to Rome was now out of the question. Out of the window went any further attempt to convince the Pope of his orthodoxy and obedience.

By the end of 613 AD he had made his decision to stand and fight. On the advice of one of Agilulf's advisers, a man named Jucundus, a royal charter was proclaimed granting land for the foundation of a new monastery at Bobbio in the valley of the River Trebbia (O'Fiaich, 1990, p. 52). The choice of Bobbio was tantamount to a declaration of war. It was not just a vacant and convenient bit of a real estate. Bobbio had several things going for it.

To begin with it was in a position of great beauty with the convenience of a wild mountainous backdrop where Columban could, as was his custom, find for himself a secluded hermitage in a cave not too far distant from his monastery.

But that was not all. Bobbio was of great symbolic importance. By choosing Bobbio Columban was effectively giving a great big sock in the face to Rome, for Bobbio was the second site in Italy where St Peter was known to have founded a church of his own. The Church at Bobbio, like the Church in Rome, was still called after him — St Peter's.

The Pope's principal claim to authority within the European church had always been that he was the heir of St Peter — a claim that rankled somewhat with the Celts who looked to St John as their principal authority. However they conceded that the Church in Rome had indeed been founded by Peter and contained his sepulchre and for this reason, and for this reason alone, they were prepared to give precedence to the Patriarch of Rome.

By choosing Bobbio Columbanus was sending out a very deliberate message to his opponents further south. He was not simply setting himself up as Abbot of the new monastery but as an alternative authority to the Pope in Rome. Nearby — another piece of potent symbolism — Hannibal had trounced the Romans. Furthermore Bobbio was on the pilgrim path to Rome. Its guest-house we are told attracted many travellers who sometimes stayed to become residents. In other words it was a great place to poach supporters from the Pope.

Columbanus, despite his seventy years, threw himself into the project with great enthusiasm, even carrying the timbers for the new building himself.

Diplomatic missions passed secretly between the Lombards and the Franks and it appears that not a few of them passed through Bobbio via the wandering monks. We know that one came headed by the new Abbot of Luxeuil, Columban's old friend Eustasius, bringing gold from Lothar, ostensibly to fund the building of the new monastery. This might publicly appear to be simply an expression of Lothar's piety or his affection for his old mentor, but he also had a political interest in funding the opposition to the Pope and the Emperor in Constantinople. Anything that would undermine their authority would be beneficial to his own claim (Jonas, p. 30).

It seems also that behind the benefaction was an unofficial offer of alliance between the Franks and the Lombards. It seems that around this time negotiations were in progress and, although Agilulf at this point still wished to keep this a secret, through the good offices of Columbanus, a peace treaty was eventually formally agreed.

As 613 AD moved into 614 AD the news came that Jerusalem had fallen and the Emperor Heraclius had to brace himself for more bad news.

In Burgundy Theodemanda had been captured.

Chapter 17

The Fame of Mortal Life

Of course Columbanus had seen all this coming, apparently in a quite literal way. Jonas records how while still in Switzerland he had seen in a vision the outcome of the battle between the brothers.

> On the day of the battle, Columban, who was with Chagnoald in the forest near Bregenz, had a vision of the slaughter. "Father", exclaimed the young monk, "pray for Theodebert that he may obtain the victory over Theoderic, our common enemy." "You give advice that is foolish and contrary to the Gospel", Columbanus reproved him. "The Lord asked us to pray for our enemies" (Jonas, p. 29).

Apart from the Christian homily demonstrating Columban's impeccable theology this story is instructive. It makes it very clear that from the point of view of the Celtic monks it was Theoderic who was the enemy and his allies also. Which makes it unlikely that the queen who was captured was his aged grandmother Brunhild who had always been close to Columban and his loyal supporter. Besides Brunhild we know had gone to live with her other grandson Theodebert because of her disgust at the influence of Theoderic's mistress. We do not hear of it but it is more than likely that she had by this date simply passed away in old age.

The queen who was captured, although she might by now have taken the name Brunhild to bolster her authority, was the one I have chosen to call Theodemanda. She was probably captured in the spring of 614 AD. The dates are quite vague in the chronicles but battles were normally fought in the spring. It is Jonas we have to thank for the error in identification because he tells us that following Theoderic's death

> Brunhilda then placed the crown on the head of his son Sigibert. But Lothar remembered Columban's prophecy and gathered together an army to reconquer the land which belonged to him. Sigibert with his troops advanced to attack him but was captured together with his five brothers and great-grandmother Brunhilda by Lothar. The latter had the boys killed one by one but Brunhilda he had first placed on a camel in mockery and so exhibited her to all her enemies round about then she was bound to the tails of wild horses and thus perished wretchedly.

Fredegar in his chronicle follows Jonas and thus the noble Brunhild of Gregory's History has acquired a very unsavoury reputation. But Theoderic's grandmother had no legal right to crown her great-grandson. It is her *granddaughter* who is able to do so staking her claim through her direct descent from Childebert, being his only surviving child male or female, under the Justinian Code.

However, it is worth noting two elements in Jonas' account. One is that the family names had evidently been handed down to the next generation. Sigibert was the great-grandfather of the son of Theoderic.

The other is that the choice of names is highly significant. This is the first time Theoderic's son is referred to by name and it may be that both the Queen and her eldest son acquired their names on this accession. We have learned from Gregory that the earlier Brunhild and Sigibert were highly regarded and respectable rulers. It was not unusual at this period for a ruler with a dodgy reputation to seek to gain political respectability by adopting the name of a more respectable ancestor.

Theodemanda/Brunhild and her son Sigibert had a problem. Although they had the support of the Roman nobility in Gaul, the Frankish nobility were not united in their support. The emphasis on these Frankish names suggests an attempt to keep the Frankish aristocracy on board. Prior to their defeat and capture Lothar managed to draw the

Frankish nobility back over to his side which enabled him to achieve his victory.

The fate of this second Brunhild is shocking to modern readers. She was flogged, stripped naked, tortured for several days, exhibited on the back of a camel then tied by her hair to the tails of wild horses which galloped in different directions until it tore her body to pieces after which it was burnt like offal outside Lothar's camp.

If this account is accurate it makes it even more unlikely that the elder Brunhild was the captive for not only did Lothar hold her in affection but at eighty it is unlikely that she would have survived the first part of the execution never mind made it to the later stages.

The choice of a camel rather than a horse on which to exhibit the fallen queen is an important one. Camels were hardly common in 7th century Europe. A camel is a beast associated with the East — we would associate it with Arabs but in the 7th century in northern Europe it would have been a symbol of the Eastern Empire which still included Egypt, Libya and most of what we would now tend to think of as Arab lands. This fact alone tells us that Theodemanda was allied to Constantinople.

Her manner of execution — the pulling apart by wild horses — was reserved for the highest of high treason. It was not a common form of execution at all. She had not only been guilty of the murder of a Frankish king and a kinsman of Lothar, whose death he was honour bound to avenge, she had been in league with a foreign power. The extremity of the punishment indicates the seriousness with which her action was regarded. It was simply unforgiveable.

She was never married to Theoderic, or at any rate their union appears never to have been recognised by the rest of the family and her sons were regarded as illegitimate so she couldn't put up the defence Guntram had accepted for Fredegund — that she was the queen and the mother of the legitimate heir.

Jonas makes the point that Lothar is conducting the war on the grounds that he is reconquering lands that belong to him. As we have seen this was only the case under Frankish law. Theodemanda and her sons were claiming rights of inheritance under the Justinian Code. This explains the rather curious reference in Fredegar's Chronicle in which he insists that Theodebert was not Childebert's legitimate son but the son of a concubine and one of his gardeners (Thorpe, 1974, p. 470). This scurrilous suggestion surfaces long after his death. At the time of his birth Gregory mentions no such rumours. His mother could not have been a concubine but Childebert's lawful wife. Nor it appears did Childebert harbour any doubts about his eldest son's paternity or legitimacy. Gregory tells us that when the citizens of Soissons and Meaux asked Childebert to send one of his sons to reside with them

> He promised to send his elder son Theodebert to them. He appointed counts, personal servants, major-domos and tutors to serve him and everyone else necessary for his royal household. In the month of August he sent the prince (*Ibid.*, p. 523).

Never in his lifetime had Theodebert's status as a prince been questioned so why does this story surface after his death?

One explanation bears out the theory that Theodemanda was Theoderic's half-sister and the full sister of Theodebert. Her claim to the throne under the Justinian Code rested on the fact that she was the legitimate daughter of Childebert II.

It would at this point have suited Lothar to allow a story to circulate which cast doubt on her descent. The story perhaps originally related to her paternity rather than her brother's. This would make sense as it would be something of an embarrassment to Lothar to have been forced to execute his own kinswoman for treason. Merovingian men did not normally deal with the women in their family in quite such a brutal fashion. A scandal which allowed Lothar to repudiate any blood-tie would both ease his conscience and undermine any suggestion that the sons of Theoderic had a legitimate claim under the Justinian Code.

The fact that Gregory does not mention that Childebert had a daughter or Theodebert a sister is not in itself surprising as he very rarely mentions the birth of female offspring. Only where, as in the case of Chilperic's daughters, they play an important part in the story do we learn of their existence and Theodemanda did not come to the fore until after Gregory's death. On the whole all the evidence points to Theoderic's mistress and Queen (who may or may not have been called Brunhild) being his half-sister and the sister of Theodebert.

Columban is known to have written to Lothar at this time and it is always assumed that his letter was by way of a rebuke for the extremity of the sentence[1] but given the number of devils Jonas associates with Theodemanda we should perhaps not be too quick to make this assumption. Columban may just as well have been sending his congratulations as reproving his former charge. Indeed he had far more reason to congratulate him than otherwise.

With Lothar now in full command of all the Frankish kingdoms Columban was invited to return to the Neustrian court. Lothar seems to have continued to yearn for the company of his mentor but Columbanus was unable to make the journey.

> To the king [Jonas tells us], he sent a letter full of good advice and begged him to extend his royal protection and assistance to the brethren at Luxeuil. The king received the letter with great joy as a precious gift and as a pledge of his friendship with the man of God. Nor did he forget the latter's request but showed his favour in every way to the monastery, gave it yearly revenues, increased its estates in every direction as the venerable Eustasius desired and assisted its inmates in every way he could (Jonas, p. 31).

Probably his health was beginning to fail but also by the summer of 614 AD the monastery at Bobbio was up and running and his strategy of challenging the Pope in Italy was beginning to succeed.

He chose therefore to stay at Bobbio and make his last stand. He must have had some premonition that his life was coming to a close as the autumn began to draw in because his last act as Abbot was to send the staff which had accom-

---

[1]   This letter is no longer extant.

panied him through all his wanderings and was a sign of his authority to his old friend Gall, still living a hermit's life in Switzerland.

Gall accepted this gratefully as a sign of reconciliation and forgiveness — he was now able to celebrate communion as it was evidence that Columbanus had lifted his ban. But perhaps, since he knew Columban of old, he saw it also as the passing on of a life's mission, even a sign of admission — and he would have known how hard it would be for Columban to admit he was wrong — that he had been right.

Columbanus had never been invited to Rome. The Pope had never agreed to hold a synod to allow the Celts to put their case in open debate. Despite all his efforts to reach a rapprochement with the Roman bishops they clearly were not interested in reconciliation with the Celtic Church.

There are two grottoes still pointed out in the mountainside above Bobbio as places to which Columban used to retire to pray, study and meditate for to the end of his life he continued to practice the anchorite way whenever he was able to set aside his responsibilities to the community and his involvement in international politics.

To the north-east of Bobbio is a small cave about five feet long and seven feet high in a steep cliff-face some five hundred feet above the Trebbia valley from which a foaming torrent dashes down into the river below. This place was called La Spanna from an open hand carved on the rock to mark the border of the province of Pavia.

The other grotto to the south-west of Bobbio is now a large cave twenty feet long and eight feet high. In Columban's day a small oratory dedicated to St Michael stood beside it. According to tradition the Abbot died here alone (O'Fiaich, 1990, p. 137).

Consequently we do not have in Jonas' Life the usual climactic deathbed scene with the customary description of the transfiguration one associates with the lives of saints. Was Columbanus met by angels? Did he finally achieve the transition to Christ he had worked towards all his life?

We have to make do with a secondary account. Jonas tells us that in the early hours of Sunday 23rd November 615 AD as Columbanus breathed his last and, we hope, passed peacefully into the afterlife he so longed for, hundreds of miles to the north Gall woke his deacon Magnoald and told him to prepare everything necessary for the celebration of Mass, the very thing Columbanus had forbidden him to do before his life ended in his rage and disappointment.

Magnoald was understandably astonished but Gall told him, "I have learnt in a vision that my Lord and Father Columban has passed from the miseries of this life to the joys of Paradise this day. Therefore I must say Mass for the rest of his soul."

As soon as Mass was over Magnoald was sent to Bobbio where he found everything had happened just as Gall had related from his vision.

He stayed overnight, made the 8-day journey back to St Gallen (not called that then of course while Gall was still living) bearing a letter from the monks of Bobbio describing Columbanus' last hours and his last request and the staff of office to be handed on to Gall, appointing him effectively the leader of the Celtic Church in Europe.

Gall treasured it for 15 years until his own death around 630 AD.

It was for centuries preserved in the abbey church of the monastery of St Gall and was described as being at Fussen as late as 1748. By that time it was no more than three feet long, barely a walking stick, and mounted in a silver shrine but by then it had already served its purpose. The Protestant Reformation had swept across Europe following the trail that Columban had blazed nearly a thousand years before (*Ibid.*, pp. 54–5).

How should we sum up Columban's life? He did it himself so I can do no better than quote his own words beautifully translated by Cardinal O'Fiaich.

This is Columban's acrostic verse to Hunaldus. In Latin the first letters spell their respective names, but here it is in English.

> In countless ways life's seasons disappear
> They all pass by, the months complete a year,
> With every moment, tottering age draws near.

Into eternal life that you may go
Spurn now the sweet deceits of life below,
Soft lust can upright virtue overthrow.
No breast to blind desire and greed is cold,
A mind rapt up in cares can't judge a deed,
To gold all silver yields, to virtue gold,
The highest peace is but to seek one's need.

This trifling poem I've sent you; read it oft,
Give entrance in your ears to these my words,
Let not some whim seduce you, transient, soft,
See how the power is brief of kings and lords.

Quickly the fame of mortal life is gone.
Pardon my words, perhaps they're overdone;
Whatever is too much, remember, shun! (*Ibid.* pp. 96–97)

He had seen for himself how briefly the power of kings and
lords glittered, how transient was the glory of popes and
emperors, but he may have been pleasantly surprised to
find that the fame of his own mortal life was not after all
such a brittle thing as he had supposed.

Bibiliography

Boyton, Henry, *Dictionary of Irish Biography* (Gill & Macmillan, 1978).

Brown, Michelle P., *How Christianity came to Britain and Ireland* (Lion Hudson, 2006).

Cahill, Thomas, *How the Irish saved Civilisation* (Sceptre, 1995).

Catholic Encyclopedia, Vol IV, *Entry for St Columbanus* (1908, New York (internet)).

Chadwick, Nora, *The Celts* (Pelican, 1970).

Chadwich, Owen, *A History of Christianity* (Weidenfeld & Nicolson, 1995).

Colgrave, Bertram (trans.), Bede, *The Ecclesiastical History of the English People*, ed. Judith McClure/Roger Collins (Oxford University Press, 1999).

Columbanus, *Sermons and Letters* (Cork University Library website).

Collins, Roger, *Macmillan History of Europe – Early Mediaeval Europe 300–1000* (Macmillan, 1999).

Coulson, J. (ed.), *The Saints: A Concise Biographical Dictionary* (Burns & Oates, London, 1958).

Davies, John, *A History of Wales* (Penguin, 2007).

Deansley, Margaret, *The Pre-Conquest Church in England* (Adam and Charles Black, 1961).

Durant, Will, *The Age of Faith* (Simon and Schuster, New York, 1950).

Ehrman, Bart D., *Lost Scriptures* (Oxford University Press, New York, 2003).

Filbee, Marjorie, *Celtic Cornwall* (Constable, 1996).

Highet, G., *The Classical Tradition* (Oxford University Press, 1959).

Hill, Jonathan, *The New Lion Handbook of the History of Christianity* (Lion Hudson, 2007).

Johnson, Donald S., *Phantom Islands of the Atlantic* (Souvenir Press, 1997).

Jonas of Susa, *Life of Columbanus*, trans. D.C. Munro, from Mabillon 2nd vol of Acta Sanctorum OSB (Fordham University website).

Lapidge, Michael (ed.), *Columbanus: Studies on the Latin Writings* (Boydell Press, 1997).

Lehane, Brendan, *Early Celtic Christianity* (Continuum, 2005).

McManners, John (ed.),*The Oxford Illustrated History of Christianity* (Oxford University Press, 1990).

Malory, Thomas, *Mort d'Arthur*, ed. Tom Griffith (Wordsworth, 1996).

Matz, Terry, *The Daybook of Saints* (Mitchell Beazley, 2000).

Mango, Cyril, *By antium : The Empire of the New ome* (Phoenix, 2005).

Merton & Barber, *The Travels and Adventures of the Three Princes of Serendip* (Princeton, 2004).

Mitchell, G.D. (ed.), *A Dictionary of Sociology* (Routledge & egan Paul, 1968).

Morton, H.V., *In search of Wales* (Methuen & Co, 1936).

Northumbrian Community, *Celtic Daily Prayer* (Collins, 2005).

O'Fiaich, Cardinal Tomas, *Columbanus in his Own Words* (Veritas, 1990).

Pagden, Anthony, *Peoples and Empires Europeans and the rest of the world from Antiquity to the Present* (Phoenix, 2002).

Pennick, Nigel, *The Celtic Saints* (Thornsons (Harper Collins, 1997).

Pine-Coffin, R.S. (trans.), St. Augustine, *Confessions* (Penguin, 1961).

Seaborne, Malcolm, *Celtic Crosses of Britain and Ireland* (Shire Archaeology, 2009).

Spearing, A.C. (trans.), Anon, *The Cloud of nknowing and other works* (Penguin, 2001).

Stokes, Whitley (eds.), *Lives of the Saints from the Book of Lismore* (Clarendon Press, Oxford, 1890).

Thomas, Ruth, *South Wales* (John Bartholomew & Son Ltd, 1977).

Thorpe, Lewis (trans. and ed.), Gregory of Tours, *The History of the Franks* (Penguin, 1974).

Thurston, Hubert and Donald Attwater (eds.), *Butler's Lives of the Saints* Palm Publishers, 1956).

Watts, Victor (trans.) Boethius, *Consolations of Philosophy* (Penguin, 1999).

Welch, Robert (ed.), *Oxford Companion to Irish Literature* (Clarendon Press, Oxford, 1996).

Whitelock, Dorothy (ed.), *English Historical Documents ol 1 c 00–10 Letter regory the reat to Theoderic and Theodebert Anglo Saxon Chronicle Life of St Coelfrith Abbot of arrow* (Eyre Methuen, 1979).

Woods, Richard J., *The Spirituality of the Celtic Saints* (Orbis Books, New York, 2000).

Index

Ado 173

Aedan mac Gabrain, King of Dalriada 60

Aedh 130

Aethelbert, King of Kent 144-5

Aethelfrith 152-3

Aggripinus, Bishop of Como 186-190, 192, 198-99

Agilan 74-75, 197

Agilulf, King of Lomardy 196-99, 202, 204

Anatolius of Laodicea 124, 127, 147

Annegray (Anagrates) 13, 63-64, 107, 112, 119, 121, 122, 129, 139, 142, 178

Ansovald 105

Arthur, Celtic God 42

Arthur, High King of Britain 6-7, 10, 42, 86

Athanagild, King of Spain 88, 94-95

Attala 165, 170, 174, 184, 186

Audo 104

Audoan 173

Audovera 94, 96, 100, 144-145, 151-153, 163

Augustine of Canterbury, St. 10, 20, 120, Aurelian, Paul 11, 50

Bangor Iscoed 10-11, 20, 150-151, 153

Bangor, NI 16, 18, 19, 26, 60, 62, 124, 134, 146-7, 150

Basina, daughter of Chilperic 100

Baudulf 167

Bede, The Venerable 19, 30, 120, 132, 139, 145, 151-3, 155, 163

Beppolen 105

Bertechar, Count 168, 179

Bobbio 2, 9, 28, 184, 202-3, 209-11

Bobelin 174

Boniface III, Pope 155, 159 Footnote 163

Boniface IV, Pope 77-78, 163, 164, 186-190, 192, 197, 200-201

Bregenz 178, 182, 199, 205

Brendan, St. 55, 62

Brochfail Ysgrithrog (Brocmail) 153

Brunhild, wife of Sigibert 88-89, 94-98, 105, 108-109, 141-142, 157-159, 160, 162, 201, 205-207

Cadoc, St. 11, 49

Caramtoc, Abbot of Saulcy 121

Cassian, John 24

Chagneric 173, 174

Chagnoald 173-174, 182, 205

Charibert 87

Childebert II, King of Austrasia 71, 74, 86, 96, 98, 100, 102-104, 108-112, 141, 142, Footnote 158, 182, 196, 200, 202, 206, 208

Chilperic, King of Neustria 70-73, 75-76, 79-83, 86-89, 91 – 111, 140, 141, 147, 157, 199, 209

Clonard 13, 134

Clovis, King of the Franks 86, 87, 158, 179

Clovis, son of Chilperic 96-97, 99, 100

Columba of Iona (Columcille) 1, 2, 11, 29, 47, 56-61, 63 Footnote 67, 179

Columba the Younger Footnote 2

Columbanus 1-3, 5-13, 16-19, 25-26, 28-29, 37-39, 41, 44, 48-9, 52, 54-57, 60-63, 65, 67 -68, 70, 77-78, 80-82, 85-86, 90-92, 102, 109, 112, 114-115, 117, 119, 120-133, 135-136, 138-139, 142-144, 146-150, 154, 155-160, 162-170, 172-173, 176-180, 182-184,

186-190, 193-199, 201-206, 209-211
Comgall, St. 11, 18, 37, 54, 58, 60, 62, 134, 146
Cyril of Alexandria 190

Desideratus 100
Desiderius, Bishop of Vienne 173
Desiderius, General 109-110
Diarmid, High King of Tara 56-57
Diecola 167
Dionysius Exiguus 146
Domoal 123, 129, 168

Eberulf 104
Eriugena, John Scottus 125, 126
Ermenburga 158-159
Ethelburga (Bertha), Daughter of Charibert 145
Eunoc 168
Eustasius 174, 182, 203, 209
Evans, Rev. Theophilus 150, 151, 153

Faileuba 141
Fara 139, 173
Finnian of Clonard 11, 13, 29, 115, -117, 134
Fontaine 63, 122, 129, 139, 142, Footnote 148, 178
Fredegar 141, 160, 206-7
Fredegund, Queen of Neustria 73, 80, 88-89, 93-97, 99-106, 108-110, 142, 160, 199, 207
Fridiburga Footnote 183

Gall, St. 167-168, 177-178, 183, 210-211
Galswinth 94-96, 159
Germanus of Auxerre, St. 25, 41
Germanus, St. Bishop of Paris 89
Gildas 11, 13, 50, Footnote 148
Gregory the Great, Pope Footnote 7, 10, 77, 120, 124, 126-127, 132, 143-145, 147-148, 153, 155, 156, 186
Gregory, Bishop of Tours 24, 64, 70-77, 80-81, 83, 85, 88-89, 91-94, 97, 99, 103, 105, 107-111 Footnote 119, 129, 140-141, 146-147, 160, 168-169, 195, 197, 206, 208, 209
Gundovald 85, 87, 109-111
Guntram Boso, Duke, 97
Guntram, King of Burgundy 68, 70-71, 74, 85, 87-89, 93, 95, 98,

100, Footnote 101, 103-105, 107-111, 141, 142, 157, 160, 202, 207
Gunzo, Duke 182

Heracleides Ponticus 125
Heraclius, Emperor 164, 200, 201, 204
Hermagoras of Temnos 126, 127, 191, 192
Herpo 97
Honoratus, St. 24
Hunaldus 4

Illtud 11, 49
Inishmurray 14, 116

Jonas of Susa 9, 17, 29, 48, 54-55, 62, 64, 68, 70, 81, 114, 121, 123, 130, 131, 143, 157, 158, 159, 160, 162, 163, 166-170, 172-174, 178-180, 188, 204-207, 209, 210
Jucundus 202
Justinian, Emperor (Justinian Code) 144, Footnote 158, 180, 181, 182, 186, 189, 206, 208

Laurentius 10, 154
Leoparius, Bishop of Tours 169
Lerins 24
Leuvigild, King of Spain 74, 80
Lothar I, King of the Franks 85, 87, 94, 101, 103, 110 145, 158
Lothar II, King of Neustria 68, 70, 107, 141, 142, 143, 162, 167, 168, 172, 173, 180, 190, 200-204, 206-209
Lua 168, 169
Luxeuil 63, 119, 122, 129, 139, 142, 143, 147, 154, 164, 166, 167, 170, 173, 174, 177, 178, 183, 184, 209

Magnoald 211
Mallulf, Bishop of Senlis 102
Marculf 121
Martianus Capella 125
Martin of Tours, St. 24, 25, 169
Maurice Tiberius, Emperor 110-111, Melantius, Bishop of Rouen 108
Mellitus, Bishop of London 163
Merovech, son of Chilperic 96-99, 104
Meton 124
Molaisse, St. 57, 137

Mummolus, General 109-110,
Footnote 158, 164, 196

Nestorius 189, 190-192
Niall of the Nine Hostages 6-7
Nicetius, Bishop of Besancon 168

Palladius 25, 41
Patrick, St. 11, 24-25, 40, 44, 45
Pelagius (Morgan), British Monk
77, 150, 151, 189, 194
Pelagius II, Pope 77, 80
Phocas, Emperor 164
Praetextatus, Bishop of Rouen
98-99, 105-106, 108
Ptolemy (*Author of the Almagest*)
125

Ragamund, Count 168, 170
Recared, son of the King of Spain
74, 80
Rigunth, daughter of Chilperic 74,
80, 104, 109, 110
Romachar, Bishop of Coutances
106

Sabinian, Pope 155, 156, 159
Samson of Dol 11, 50
Samson, son of Chilperic 99
Schuman, Robert 1, 2
Sigibert (Companion to
Columbanus) 184
Sigibert, King of Austrasia
Footnote 68, 70-71, 87-89, 93-97,
100, 141, 142, 206

Sigibert, son of Theoderic Footnote
183, 206
Sinell, St., 11, 16
Skellig Michael 13
Sofronius, Bishop of Nantes 170
Strabo, Walafrid 178

Theodebert, son of Chilperic 88, 96
Theodebert, son of Childebert 141,
143, 157, 158, 159, 162, 172, 173,
174, 179, 180, 182, 184, 202, 205,
208
Theodelinda, Queen of Lombardy
196, 198, 200
Theodemanda 157-158, 160, 164,
173, 180, 182, Footnote 183, 198,
200- 202, 204, 205-209
Theoderic, son of Childebert 100,
141- 143, 158-160, 162-164, 166,
168-169, 172, 174, 179, 180- 182,
Footnote 183, 184, 199, 200, 202,
205- 209
Theodore, Bishop of Marseilles
109, 110, 111
Tiberius II, Emperor 76, 77, 110
Footnote 158

Ulfilas 188, 198
Ursicinius 174, 177

Victor of Aquitaine 146
Victorius 127, 146, 147
Vulfoliac Footnote 119

Willimar 177